FLOYD CLYMER'S MOTORCYCLIST'S LIBRARY

The Book of the

ARIEL LEADER AND ARROW

A PRACTICAL GUIDE TO THE HANDLING AND MAINTENANCE OF ALL 1958–66 ARIEL 247 C.C. PARALLEL TWIN TWO-STROKE MODELS

BY

W. C. HAYCRAFT

F.R.S.A.

ANNOUNCEMENT

By special arrangement with the original publishers of this book, Sir Isaac Pitman & Son, Ltd., of London, England, we have secured the exclusive publishing rights for this book, as well as all others in THE MOTORCYCLIST'S LIBRARY.

Included in THE MOTORCYCLIST'S LIBRARY are complete instruction manuals covering the care and operation of respective motorcycles and engines; valuable data on speed tuning, and thrilling accounts of motorcycle race events. See listing of available titles elsewhere in this edition.

We consider it a privilege to be able to offer so many fine titles to our customers.

FLOYD CLYMER
Publisher of Books Pertaining to Automobiles and Motorcycles

2125 W. PICO ST.   LOS ANGELES 6, CALIF.

INTRODUCTION

Welcome to the world of digital publishing ~ the book you now hold in your hand, while unchanged from the original edition, was printed using the latest state of the art digital technology. The advent of print-on-demand has forever changed the publishing process, never has information been so accessible and it is our hope that this book serves your informational needs for years to come. If this is your first exposure to digital publishing, we hope that you are pleased with the results. Many more titles of interest to the classic automobile and motorcycle enthusiast, collector and restorer are available via our website at www.VelocePress.com. We hope that you find this title as interesting as we do.

NOTE FROM THE PUBLISHER

The information presented is true and complete to the best of our knowledge. All recommendations are made without any guarantees on the part of the author or the publisher, who also disclaim all liability incurred with the use of this information.

TRADEMARKS

We recognize that some words, model names and designations, for example, mentioned herein are the property of the trademark holder. We use them for identification purposes only. This is not an official publication.

INFORMATION ON THE USE OF THIS PUBLICATION

This manual is an invaluable resource for the classic motorcycle enthusiast and a "must have" for owners interested in performing their own maintenance. However, in today's information age we are constantly subject to changes in common practice, new technology, availability of improved materials and increased awareness of chemical toxicity. As such, it is advised that the user consult with an experienced professional prior to undertaking any procedure described herein. While every care has been taken to ensure correctness of information, it is obviously not possible to guarantee complete freedom from errors or omissions or to accept liability arising from such errors or omissions. Therefore, any individual that uses the information contained within, or elects to perform or participate in do-it-yourself repairs or modifications acknowledges that there is a risk factor involved and that the publisher or its associates cannot be held responsible for personal injury or property damage resulting from the use of the information or the outcome of such procedures.

WARNING!

One final word of advice, this publication is intended to be used as a reference guide, and when in doubt the reader should consult with a qualified technician.

PREFACE

THE 247 c.c. parallel twin two-stroke Ariel Leader and Arrow supersede the former Ariel four-stroke range and are high performance modern machines which should give excellent service provided they are handled well and regular maintenance is attended to as advised in this handbook. Its purpose is to assist you to obtain the maximum pleasure, mileage, m.p.h., m.p.g., and m.p.£ from your mount.

The Leader and Arrow are of very similar general design, but there are some important differences, except in regard to their engines, which are identical apart from carburettor settings. *All instructions except where otherwise stated apply to both models.*

If you are a mechanic and have the necessary facilities you can tackle major overhaul work. An excellent Ariel Workshop Manual is obtainable (price £1 10s.) from Ariel Motors Ltd of Armoury Road, Birmingham, 11 (Phone: Birmingham, Victoria 5643). Many special service tools are also available. The average motor-cyclist has not the time, experience or facilities to tackle major dismantling and overhaul and should approach the nearest appointed Ariel dealer. The author has for the reasons just mentioned not attempted to deal with major dismantling and overhaul.

In conclusion the author is indebted to Ariel Motors Ltd (and various accessory firms) for providing some technical data and for according permission to reproduce certain illustrations.

W.C.H.

CONTENTS

CHAP.   PAGE

I. HANDLING YOUR MACHINE 1
II. CORRECT LUBRICATION 20
III. THE AMAL CARBURETTOR 27
IV. THE LUCAS LIGHTING SYSTEM 37
V. GENERAL MAINTENANCE 47
   Index 75

CHAPTER I

HANDLING YOUR MACHINE

IN this chapter it is only possible to deal very briefly with actual riding, legal matters, etc. The information given is for those who have, or are about to purchase, an Ariel Leader or Arrow and have had little or no experience with these machines. As regards actual riding on the road, the author emphasizes two absolutely essential points: firstly read and thoroughly digest the contents of *The Highway Code*; secondly besides purchasing a good warm coat and weatherproof coat, make sure that you buy a well fitting and good make of proprietary *crash* helmet. With modern traffic conditions even the most experienced and careful rider can meet with an accident through no fault of his own.

The Ariel 247 c.c. Two-strokes. For many years Ariel Motors Ltd. concentrated on a range of excellent four-stroke models, but the four-stroke range ceased at the end of August, 1960, and the Ariel Leader, the Arrow, and a sports version of the latter have since comprised the complete Ariel motor-cycle range. These machines have proved extremely successful and are in many respects of revolutionary design. So successful and popular have they proved, that the makers have found it quite unnecessary to make appreciable alterations in their design each year. This is very beneficial both in regard to prices and spare parts.

Having an engine capacity not exceeding 250 c.c., the Leader and Arrow are suitable for learner riders and because of their performance, economy, reliability, and easy maintenance both models should also appeal to experienced riders. Both models are easy to handle and have good steering and road-holding qualities. The exhaust noise is quiet and pleasant. Maximum speed is approximately 70 m.p.h. Petrol consumption at 40 m.p.h. averages 80–90 miles per gallon.

The Ariel Leader. Introduced in 1958, this machine has a 247 c.c. parallel-twin two-stroke engine with unit construction of the engine and four-speed gearbox. Both primary and secondary chains are completely enclosed. Lucas electrical equipment is fitted throughout, and the machine has a modern Amal monobloc type carburettor with cold starting device. Other prominent features are the sturdy box-type "chassis" (*see* Fig. 3), the unusual type front forks, and the excellent weather protection, as may be seen in Fig. 1. The total weight is about 300 lb.

FIG. 1. OFF-SIDE VIEW OF THE 247 C.C. TWO-STROKE ARIEL LEADER

The enclosure on this ultra-modern machine is quite remarkable. On the machine illustrated optional extras fitted are: pannier cases, a rear fender with reflectors, and a carrier. The dummy tank has a parcels compartment with steering head and dualseat locks inside. Beneath the hinged dualseat are the fuel tank filler cap, battery, and tool kit.

FIG. 2. NEAR-SIDE VIEW OF THE 247 C.C. TWO-STROKE ARIEL ARROW

As on the Leader, the fuel tank filler cap and battery are below the hinged dualseat. The absence of complete enclosure shows the unit construction parallel-twin engine and gearbox which is of similar design to that fitted on the Leader. Access to the rectifier is by removing the Ariel badge on the near side of the dummy tank which has a compartment housing the tool box, tyre pump, and parcels. Note the unique type trailing-link front forks. A sports version of the Arrow is available.

HANDLING YOUR MACHINE 3

The Ariel Arrow. Introduced in 1960, this mount is of similar design to the Leader and as may be seen in Fig. 2 is of handsome appearance. It has a somewhat more sporty performance and as already stated, a slightly greater maximum speed. Weather protection panels are omitted and there are some detail modifications. The total weight is about 275 lb.

A sports version of the Arrow is available. This has sports pattern

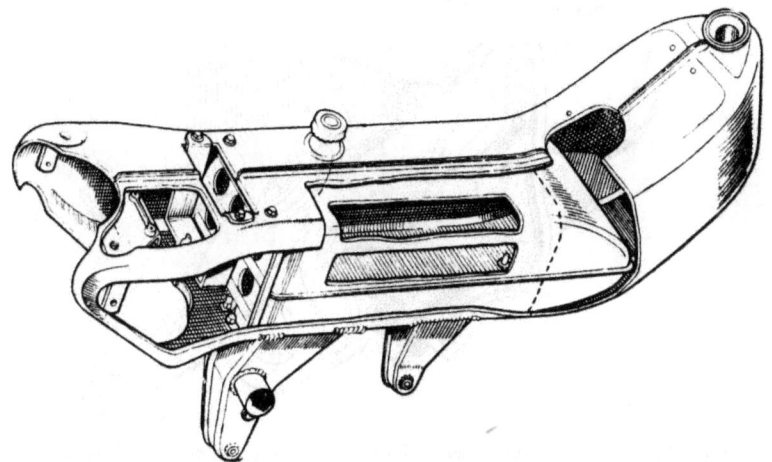

FIG. 3. A UNIQUE ARIEL FEATURE IS THE STURDY BOX-SECTION "CHASSIS" FROM WHICH ARE SUSPENDED THE UNIT-CONSTRUCTION ENGINE AND GEARBOX

Above is shown the 1962–3 version, but the general design is very similar on all 1958 and later two-stroke Ariels. It gives superb steering and road holding qualities.

(*By courtesy of "Motor Cycle," London*)

handlebars, safety ball-ended control levers, a neat flyscreen, a prop stand, folding kick-starter, and a special *de luxe* finish.

Optional Extras for the Leader. Provision is made on the instrument panel shown in Fig. 9 for fitting an eight-day clock in place of the Ariel badge; a plug-in inspection lamp, for which two-pin sockets are included; a flasher indicator warning light; a low consumption parking lamp with switch; a *neutral* warning light with switch which screws into the rear of the gearbox (*see* Fig. 4).

Other reasonably priced optional extras for fitting to a Leader machine are: a prop stand; a detachable front stand; a carrier with two straps; a chrome rear fender with reflectors; near-side and off-side mirrors for fitting to the front shield; a windscreen extension; a dualseat waterproof cover; locking pannier cases and lift-out bags to fit; and a hand case. The inclusion of all the above-mentioned extras will transform a Leader into a "Rolls Royce" type motor-cycle!

Optional Extras for the Arrow. For the Arrow and ts sports version the following optional extras are available: a windscreen; a prop stand; a front stand; a dualseat strap; a carrier with two straps; a hand case;

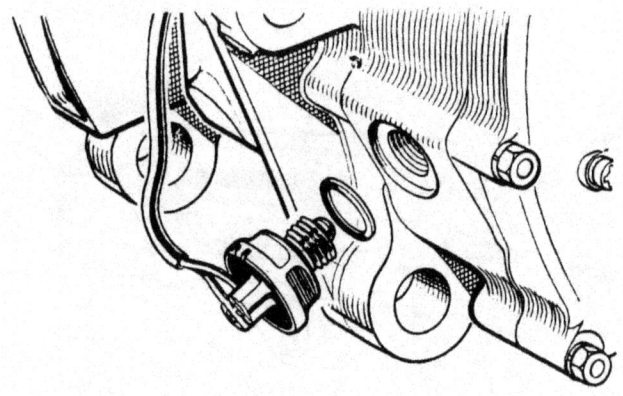

FIG. 4. WHERE AN OPTIONAL EXTRA NEUTRAL WARNING LIGHT IS FITTED TO THE LEADER INSTRUMENT PANEL THE SWITCH IS SCREWED INTO THE REAR OF THE GEARBOX

(*By courtesy of "Motor Cycle," London*)

a dualseat waterproof cover; and last but not least, a reserve petrol tap. All the above are worthwhile extras.

The Parcel Compartment on the Leader. The compartment, shown at 12 in Fig. 9, has a hinged lid which is fitted with a lock for which two keys are provided on a new machine. The key number should be noted to facilitate replacement if necessary. To open the lid, first fit the key, turn it and press. Then raise the lid. Two anti-thief devices are included inside the parcel compartment. One is a steering head lock and the other a control which locks the dualseat.

The steering head lock can be operated with the handlebars turned *fully* clockwise or anti-clockwise. To lock the steering head, move the locking lever (*see* Fig. 5) from *left to right*. When you wish to move or ride your Leader, press forward and move the locking lever from *right to left*.

A loop-ended rod located at the rear on the near side of the parcel

HANDLING YOUR MACHINE 5

compartment is used for locking or unlocking the dualseat to prevent or obtain access to the fuel tank filler cap, tool kit, or battery. To unlock the dualseat, pull on the loop-ended rod. To lock the dualseat, push the loop-ended rod *fully home*. When the dualseat has been unlocked it can, of course, readily be raised or moved to its normal position.

Tool Box, Tyre Pump, and Parcel Compartment on the Arrow. On the Arrow the compartment contains a deep tool box and a tyre pump clipped on the near side. The latter is accessible after the tool box has been removed, and there is ample room for a reasonably sized parcel when the tool box is removed. To remove the tool box, remove the outer lid secured by a single screw (slacken the screw with a coin or screwdriver), slightly pull upwards and rotate the lid-retaining strap *anticlockwise*; then lift the box and strap out.

The tool box can be replaced either way round. It has a rubber bead positioned around its outer edge. Be careful not to damage this. After replacing the tool box insert the lid-retaining strap into the wider portion of the slots in the tool box sides, and rotate *clockwise*. Make sure that the *convex* side of the strap is uppermost. Afterwards replace the outer lid and tighten its securing screw.

The Ariel Handlebars. As may be seen in Fig. 9, the handlebars on the Leader have a cover which gives protection for the control cables against damage and adds neatness to the layout. The cover also ensures smooth operation of the handlebar controls and ensures that the cables do not need renewal until a very big mileage has been covered.

On the Arrow the handlebars are secured by four clamp bolts, as may be seen in Fig. 10. If the position of the handlebars is not to your satisfaction and does not give the optimum riding position, slacken the four clamp bolts slightly and adjust the handlebars to suit your requirements. Afterward retighten the four clamp bolts very securely.

The Dualseat. This should prove very comfortable, but it is a sound plan to fit a waterproof cover which is an optional extra. One never knows when it is going to rain! The dualseat can be raised by lifting it upwards from the near side. A grab strap is provided on the Leader, and a similar strap can be fitted if desired to the Arrow.

Before raising the dualseat on the Leader do not forget to release the dualseat lock provided inside the parcels compartment, assuming, of course, that the dualseat has been locked in position. This lock has been previously referred to (*see* above). Then pull out the lifting handle shown in Fig. 7 and lift up the dualseat from the near side.

Essential Legal Preliminaries. If you are under 16 you are *not* permitted to ride *any* type of motor-cycle. Before you can legally get on the road

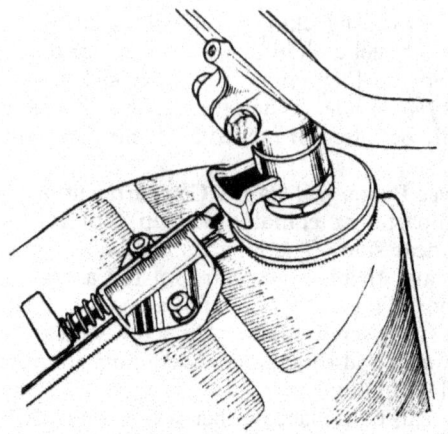

FIG. 5. THE STEERING HEAD LOCK INSIDE THE PARCEL COMPARTMENT OF THE LEADER
(*By courtesy of "Motor Cycle," London*)

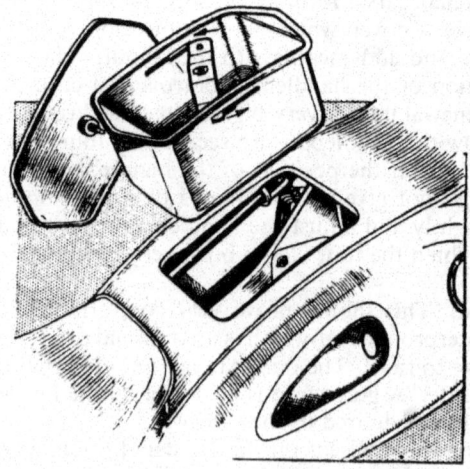

FIG. 6. ON THE ARROW REMOVAL OF THE TOOL BOX GIVES ACCESS TO THE TYRE PUMP AND PARCEL COMPARTMENT
The tool box is easily removed as described in the text.
(*By courtesy of "Motor Cycle," London*)

FIG. 7. THE PULL-OUT LIFTING HANDLE FOR THE DUALSEAT
This is provided on all Leader models.
(*By courtesy of "Motor Cycling"*)

FIG. 8. THE DUALSEAT ON THE LEADER SHOWN RAISED

1. Combined fuel tank filler cap and oil measure.
2. Lucas battery.
3. Tool-kit.
4. Dualseat lifting handle knob.
5. Knob for cold-starting device.
6. Fuel tap.

(*By courtesy of "Motor Cycle," London*)

astride a brand new or second-hand Ariel Leader or Arrow you must attend to the following essential preliminaries—

1. If you are a "learner," take out a "provisional" driving licence. It is valid for six months and the fee is 10s. The licence can be renewed as required, and the application form for each licence is D.L.I. An "L" plate must be fitted to the front and rear of the machine.

2. When you wish to apply for a driving test, fill up Form D.L.26. The fee for a driving test is £1.

3. If you are qualified to ride without "L" plates, take out a "full" driving licence. It is valid for three years and the fee is 15s. Form D.L.I.

4. Sign your driving licence.

5. Insure against all *third-party* risks and obtain the vital "certificate of insurance." With a new Leader or Arrow you cannot obtain this until the machine has been registered and a registration number is allocated to it. Pending this, obtain an insurance "cover note."

6. Obtain a registration book and a registration licence. If your machine is new or has changed hands, fill up Form R.F. 1/2. If you wish to *renew* your registration licence, fill up Form R.F. 1/A. The annual tax is £2 5s. and the fee must always be accompanied by a "certificate of insurance" or "cover note." The engine and frame numbers must be stated on Form R.F. 1/2.

7. Attach your registration licence to the front of the machine on the near side and carry your driving licence and "certificate of insurance."

8. If you hold only a "provisional" licence and carry a pillion passenger, he or she must hold a "full" current driving licence.

9. Check that your speedometer and horn are both in proper working order, and that the registration number and letters on your number plates are easily read.

Note that all the engine prefix letters and numbers are stamped on an identification plate rivetted to the "chassis." Also note that all the forms previously referred to are obtainable at any money-order post office.

CONTROLS AND FUEL REPLENISHMENT

The Ariel Controls. It is assumed that you are familiar with two-stroke general principles and understand the purpose of the controls which operate the engine and gearbox. Before starting up the parallel-twin two-stroke engine a proper understanding of all the controls is essential, especially if you are a novice. It is a good plan to sit on the dualseat and consider and memorize the effect of operating each control.

The layout of the handlebar controls on the Ariel Leader and Arrow are clearly shown in Figs. 9 and 10 respectively. It will be observed that

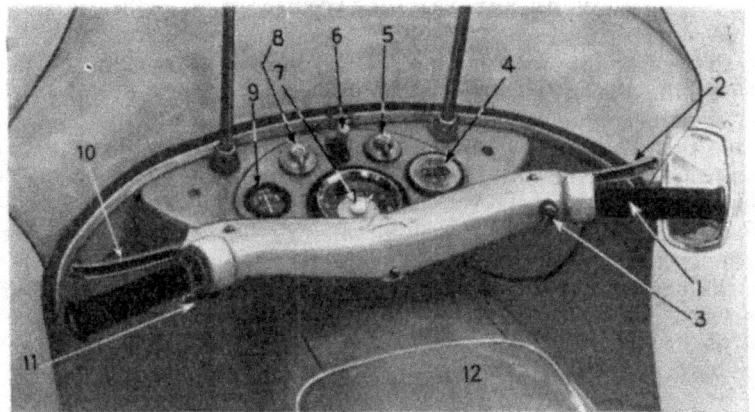

FIG. 9. LAYOUT OF INSTRUMENT PANEL AND HANDLEBAR
CONTROLS ON ARIEL LEADER

An eight-day clock may be fitted as an optional extra in place of the Ariel badge shown at 4. Other extras are available (*see* page 3).

1. Throttle twist-grip.
2. Front brake lever.
3. Horn push.
4. Ariel badge (*see* above).
5. Ignition switch.
6. Beam trimmer.
7. Speedometer.
8. Lighting switch.
9. Ammeter.
10. Clutch lever.
11. Dipper switch.
12. Parcel compartment.

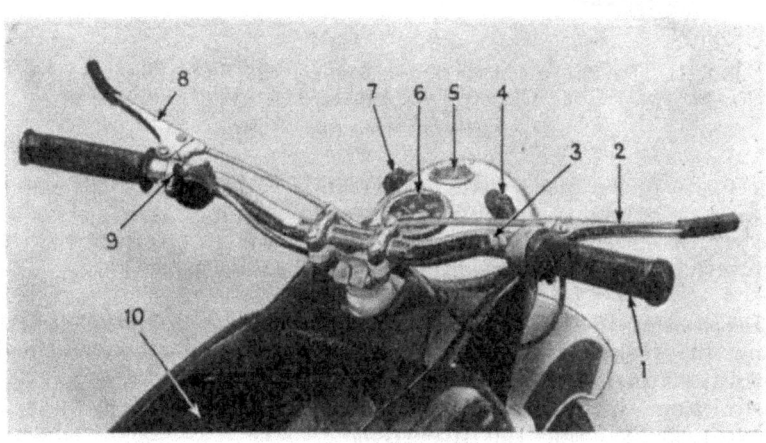

FIG. 10. HANDLEBAR CONTROL LAYOUT, AND INSTRUMENTS AND
SWITCHES ABOVE LUCAS HEADLAMP ON ARIEL ARROW

1. Throttle twist-grip.
2. Front brake lever.
3. Horn push.
4. Ignition switch.
5. Ammeter.
6. Speedometer.
7. Lighting switch.
8. Clutch lever.
9. Dipper switch.
10. Compartment for tool-box, tyre pump, and parcel.

on the Leader an instrument panel carries the ignition switch, the lighting switch, the dipper switch, and the beam trimmer, whereas on the Arrow all switches are mounted on the Lucas headlamp.

On both types of Ariel machines the rear brake pedal (*see* Fig. 15) is located just in front of the near-side footrest, the kick-starter behind the off-side footrest, and the gear-change lever (*see* Fig 13) in front of the off-side footrest. The layout of the motor-cycle controls is, of course, common to all two-stroke and four-stroke motor-cycles. There is, so far as the engine is concerned, for obvious reasons no exhaust-valve lifter and there is no air lever on the handlebars, a knob (*see* Fig. 8) is provided on the near side of the machine for operating the cold starting device on the Amal monobloc carburettor.

When Buying a New Arrow or Leader. Note that both types of machine are delivered to Ariel dealers with the Lucas type ML9E 6-volt, 12-amp battery "dry" charged. Make sure that the dealer fills the battery with

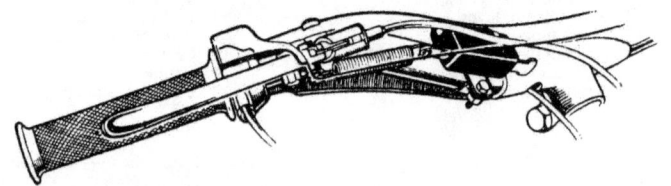

FIG. 11. TO PROVIDE ADDITIONAL SAFETY, THE FRONT BRAKE LEVER ON THE LEADER OPERATES AN INDEPENDENT STOP-LAMP SWITCH
(*By courtesy of "Motor Cycle," London*)

electrolyte in accordance with the instruction card attached to the battery. This is important, or you will have to do the job yourself. After the battery has been filled to the correct level with electrolyte it must be properly and regularly attended to as described in Chapter IV.

Replenishing Fuel Tank. To obtain access to the fuel tank filler cap, raise the dualseat (*see* page 5). Then replenish the tank with a good two-stroke petroil mixture. On a two-stroke engine to tank up with petrol alone would probably result in *ruining the engine*. The fuel tank capacity on the Leader and Arrow is *three* gallons ($2\frac{1}{4}$ gallons on standard pre-1961 models). Ariel Motors Ltd. strongly advise that the petroil mixture be made up with *premium grade petrol*. This ensures that you obtain the maximum miles per gallon and miles per hour.

During the past few years some really excellent two-stroke oils have become available. An oil measure is combined with the tank filler cap and you can, if you desire, purchase the petrol and oil separately and add

HANDLING YOUR MACHINE 11

the oil to the petrol yourself, using the oil measure (*see* Fig. 12) to insert the correct quantity of oil. Oils recommended by the engine manufacturers are as follows—

1. Castrol Two-Stroke Oil
2. Mobilmix TT
3. Esso Two-Stroke Motor Oil
4. B.P. Energol Two-Stroke Oil
5. Shell 2T Two-Stroke Oil

Note that the above-mentioned oils 1, 2, 3 are blended for easy and rapid mixing, and the correct petrol/oil ratio is 20 to 1. This is equivalent to *four* filler cap measures of oil added to each gallon of petrol. In the case of the above-mentioned oils 4, 5, the correct petrol/oil ratio is 25 to 1. This is equivalent to *three* filler cap measures of oil added to each gallon of petrol. Turn off the fuel tap and add the petrol *after* the two-stroke oil to ensure a completely homogeneous mixture.

The correct oil/petrol ratio for the petroil mixture is extremely important, and thorough mixing is also essential. Remember that on a fourstroke engine the oil and petrol in separate tanks on the motor-cycle are used for lubrication and combustion respectively; on a two-stroke engine the petroil mixture in one tank is used for both lubrication and combustion. On the Ariel two-stroke engine if an excessive amount of oil is included in the petroil mixture the probable results will be: trouble in starting the engine, fouled sparking plugs, and a choked silencer, all most undesirable and unnecessary. If in doubt about the recommended oils to use on your own particular machine, lift the dualseat up and note the advice given on a panel fitted to the underneath of the dualseat.

It is not essential to use the oil measure combined with the filler cap. Many riders, however, prefer to use the oil measure. Two-stroke motorcycles and scooters are now used in great numbers, and most garages now have modern equipment for two-stroke tank replenishment. In the author's opinion a practical and quick method of tanking up is to ride to a large garage and ask for a two-stroke *combined mixture* of petrol and oil such as Shell 2T Mixture or B.P. Zoom to be fed direct into the tank. Many big garages now have ready-mixed petroilers for injecting a Castrol, Mobiloil, Esso, B.P., or Shell petroil mixture, of the correct petrol/oil ratio. The pumps now in use have a device for ensuring that the petrol and oil ratio is as requested (20 to 1 or 25 to 1, as previously mentioned). The ratio can be altered by a device on the pump, and a ratio number, visible on the pump, indicates if the correct ratio is being supplied. See that the sight glass on the petroil pump is full before the petroil mixture is fed into your tank, and see that the ratio is correct.

At most garages the oil can be fed by a small "dispenser" into the tank *separately before* replenishing the tank with premium grade petrol. By adding oil, with a "dispenser" you can be sure that your choice of oil and petrol is used. If a 3-gallon tank is *half full*, replenish with 1½ gallons of petrol and ½ pint of two-stroke oil. This will, of course, fill the 3-gallon tank right up. To fill an empty tank right up, the quantity of petrol and oil required is, of course, 3 gallons and 1 pint respectively. Shake the machine gently from side to side to mix the petrol and oil thoroughly. Vibration when riding will ensure further thorough mixing. Filtrate two-stroke oil is rather popular among riders of two-stroke motor-cycles and the manufacturers of this oil supply special flasks.

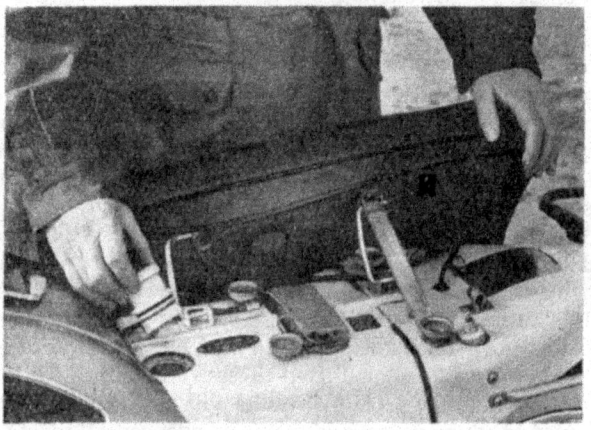

FIG. 12. REMOVING THE COMBINED TANK FILLER CAP AND OIL MEASURE

To use the oil measure the filler cap is, of course, inverted. Its position is the same on the Leader and Arrow, and the battery is similarly located on both machines. On the Arrow, shown above, the tool kit is not located under the dual-seat as on the Leader (*see* Fig. 8), but is provided in a detachable tool box as shown in Fig. 6.

(*By courtesy of "Motor Cycle," London*)

ADVICE ON RIDING

If you are a novice, learn to ride on a quiet road and keep off roads with heavy traffic until you can handle your mount well and have real confidence in your riding ability. Never forget that there are plenty of selfish car drivers on the road and they often do not take much notice of "L" plates! If you are an experienced motor-cyclist, you will handle your Ariel well very quickly.

It is assumed that you have already dealt with the necessary legal preliminaries as previously described, and have filled the tank with a suitable petroil mixture as also previously referred to. It is also assumed that the gearbox and primary chaincase have been topped up with suitable oil to the correct level (*see* pages 22, 23), and that the battery is well charged.

HANDLING YOUR MACHINE 13

Starting Up the Engine (Cold). The following is the correct procedure for starting up a *cold* Ariel Leader or Arrow two-stroke engine—

1. First check that the gear-change lever is in the *neutral* position Neutral (*see* Fig. 13) is located between first and second gears. To verify that *neutral is* engaged, rotate the rear wheel and note that this does not rotate the crankshaft assembly of the transverse twin engine. Rotation of the engine can be heard, and the compression of the pistons (when near the top-dead-centre position) felt. Alternatively push the machine off its stand and note if the motor-cycle can be readily moved backwards or forwards without resistance.

Where optional extra equipment fitted to an Ariel Leader includes a neutral indicator it is unnecessary to make the above check because with neutral engaged the warning lamp on the offside of the instrument panel shows a white light immediately you switch on the ignition. Switch off the ignition immediately you are satisfied that *neutral* is engaged.

The ignition switch has three positions marked IGN, OFF, EMG. On the Arrow the ignition switch is mounted on top of the Lucas headlamp instead of on the instrument panel (*see* Figs. 9 and 10).

2. Fill up the Amal carburettor float chamber by pulling out the fuel tap located on the near side of the motor-cycle. If there is little fuel in the tank and you have to use the reserve fuel supply, turn the tap *clockwise* and then pull out. In the case of an Arrow with a reserve type petrol tap (an optional extra) to use the reserve fuel supply, after pulling out the tap knob, turn the knob *clockwise*, and again pull it out to its full extent. The float chamber normally fills in about half a minute.

3. Pull out the knob (*see* Fig. 8) which operates the Amal carburettor cold-starting device. This knob is also on the near side of the machine just behind the petrol tap. By pulling out the knob the air supply to the carburettor is shut off completely. This is essential when starting a cold engine.

4. Open the throttle slightly by turning *inwards* the off-side twist-grip *about one-eighth of its total movement*. It is important not to open the throttle excessively.

5. Depress the kick-starter with the right foot *twice*. Where an Arrow with folding type kick-starter is concerned it is, of course, necessary first to position the kick-starter lever in its normal position.

6. Switch on the ignition by turning the ignition switch to the IGN position. Afterwards on an Arrow remove the detachable key from the ignition switch. Where the battery is discharged (indicated by the headlamp not lighting, or lighting only dimly) on a used machine, turn the ignition switch *anticlockwise* to the EMG (emergency) position.

7. With the throttle twist-grip still *one-eighth* open, standing astride your machine, depress the kick-starter *smartly*. The engine should start up immediately.

8. When the engine starts up, ease the throttle twist-grip towards the fully closed position and push in the knob operating the cold-starting device. This will allow air to enter the carburettor, and the engine should tick-over smoothly.

If the ignition switch because of a discharged battery was turned to the EMG position for starting, turn the switch *clockwise* to the normal IGN position immediately after the engine has started up. If you do not do this, some damage may result.

Do not allow the engine to run *too slowly* until it has thoroughly warmed up, and never increase the throttle opening to a *large* extent with the gear-change lever in *neutral*.

Starting Up the Engine (Warm). The engine (especially on an Arrow) cools down quickly after it has been stopped for some reason (with the gear-change lever in neutral) by closing the throttle and turning the ignition switch to the OFF position. If, however, the engine is still warm, open the throttle twist-grip appreciably more than one-eighth, switch on the ignition (*see* previous paragraph 6), open the fuel tap (*see* previous paragraph 2) if it has been closed, and start up, with the cold-starting device knob pushed home, by delivering a good kick on the kick-starter. An instant start should occur. Note the remarks (*see* previous paragraph 8) about starting up with the ignition switch in the EMG position, and about tick-over in *neutral*. It is quite easy to forget these important instructions.

Difficulty in Starting Up. On a new machine, or one that has been properly maintained, starting trouble rarely occurs, provided you follow the previous starting instructions. A likely trouble is neglected sparking plugs (*see* Chapter V). On a two-stroke engine a common and often forgotten cause of starting trouble is repeated use of the kick-starter *with the ignition switched off*. This causes both sparking plugs on a twin-cylinder engine to become wet with excessive fuel. The remedy is obvious; dry both plugs thoroughly, preferably with an air line. Parking the machine for a long period with the float chamber full can also cause starting trouble.

The use of an unsuitable petrol mixture, driving too frequently at an excessive speed, poor riding tactics, general neglect, and careless gear changing are other factors which can eventually result in starting trouble and unduly rapid wear of the engine and other parts of the motor-cycle. The penalty for such "misconduct" is unnecessary expense and dissatisfaction with a well designed and reliable machine.

HANDLING YOUR MACHINE 15

To Engage First Gear. It is assumed that you are comfortably seated with both feet firmly on the ground and that the engine is ticking-over evenly and slowly.

Disengage the clutch by pulling back the handlebar clutch lever *fully* with the left hand. Then engage 1st gear (with the right foot under the rubber) by raising the foot gear-change lever *upwards* to its *full extent*. If 1st gear does not engage readily with your Leader or Arrow stationary, move the motor-cycle slightly to and fro while maintaining light pressure on the foot gear-change rubber. Continue this action until you feel that 1st gear is engaged. Then remove your foot and place it on the footrest.

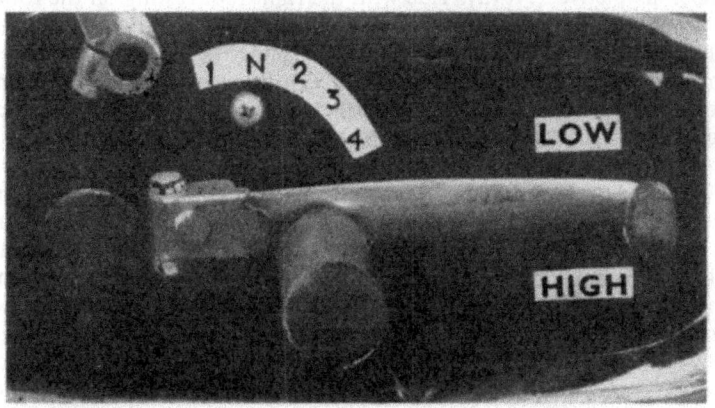

FIG. 13. THE FOOT GEAR-CHANGE LEVER ON THE FOUR-SPEED GEARBOX
All changes up to a higher gear are made by *depressing* the rubber with the toe, and all changes down to a lower gear by raising the lever. The lever automatically returns to the horizontal position after each gear change is made, and like the kick-starter lever is adjustable for position on its serrated shaft.

The gear-change lever will then automatically return to the horizontal position.

Moving Off. Open the throttle slightly by slowly turning the throttle twist-grip *inwards* and then *progressively* engage the clutch by slowly releasing the handlebar clutch lever. Do not engage the clutch suddenly, as this may cause the motor-cycle to shoot forward, especially if the engine is running rather fast. As the clutch engages and the motor-cycle increases its speed, open the throttle gradually until the speedometer needle indicates about 10 m.p.h.

Making Further Upward Gear Changes. Engage 2nd gear at about 10 m.p.h. by momentarily closing the throttle, disengaging the clutch, and *depressing* the foot gear-change lever to its full extent. Combine these three actions in *one smooth movement*. Quickly but progressively release the clutch lever when the foot gear-change lever reaches its maximum downward position, and simultaneously increase the throttle opening until the desired road speed is obtained. If there is very heavy traffic on the road keep in 2nd gear until it is safe to move faster.

Change up into 3rd and 4th (top) gears in a similar manner at about 22 m.p.h. and 27 m.p.h. respectively, and when changing up always avoid exerting excessive pressure on the rubber of the foot gear-change lever. Maintain light pressure until you fully release the clutch lever.

The art of good gear changing is quickly mastered and soon becomes almost instinctive. Always ride with the right foot resting on the footrest, never on the foot gear-change lever rubber, and with the clutch lever fully released. Movement of the gear-change lever should always be firm and deliberate, but not hurried. Avoid excessive throttle openings until a new or reconditioned engine has completed its running-in period, and ride in the gear best suited to road and traffic conditions.

Making Downward Gear Changes. Change down when your road speed drops appreciably because of road, traffic, or wind conditions. On no account allow your engine to "slog" with a high gear engaged. This applies both during and after running-in. When changing down the control movements should be made slightly more quickly than when changing up, and each gear change should be made firmly and deliberately. As when changing up, always avoid excessive pressure on the rubber of the foot-gear-change lever. Change down whenever you approach heavy slow-moving traffic or steep gradients.

When road, traffic or other conditions reduce your road speed, (with 4th (top) gear engaged) to approximately 25 m.p.h., change down into 3rd gear. When your road speed afterwards falls to about 10 m.p.h., change down into 2nd gear. Change down into 1st gear at about 5 m.p.h. Changing down is necessary to prevent the engine running too slowly. After each change down is made, adjust the throttle opening to prevent the engine running too fast. The speed of the engine automatically increases relative to the speed of the motor-cycle as each downward gear change is made, thus calling for a reduced throttle opening. Smooth and silent gear changes prolong the life of the gearbox and transmission. Remember this point.

Make each downward gear change by smartly and simultaneously disengaging the clutch, opening the throttle momentarily, and *raising* the foot gear-change pedal to its *full extent*. The foot must, of course, be positioned under the gear-change lever rubber and the use of excessive pressure should be avoided. As when making upward gear changes, you can feel when a gear is properly engaged, and the gear-change lever returns to the horizontal position after each change is made and the foot is removed.

HANDLING YOUR MACHINE

After the above method of changing down is well mastered you can learn a quicker method of changing down, used by most experienced motor-cyclists. You can rapidly change down into 1st gear by slowing down to a crawl, disengaging the clutch and making two or three full upward movements of the gear-change lever in quick succession, according to whether 3rd or 4th gear was previously engaged. Each time you raise the gear-change lever "blip" the engine by opening the throttle slightly. This method of changing down is not recommended for a novice.

Stopping the Machine. Apply the front and rear brakes simultaneously and disengage the clutch before the machine come to a standstill. Then change down into *neutral*. To do this it is necessary to change down into 1st gear before stopping, and then with the clutch disengaged, slightly and very gently *depress* the foot-gear-change lever. Do not press the lever to its full extent, otherwise you will miss *neutral* and engage 2nd gear. A light touch is necessary, and be careful to re-engage the clutch gradually in case 2nd gear has been accidentally engaged. To stop the engine, close the throttle and switch off the ignition. When you park or garage your mount, always leave the ignition switch in the OFF position. This is important.

Advice on Use of Brakes. Careless use of the Ariel brakes can land you in hospital and put a brake on your normal activities. Note the following advice—

1. Keep the brakes properly adjusted (*see* page 65).
2. Throttle right down before applying the brakes, and change down into a lower gear if necessary.
3. Use both brakes *simultaneously*. Ariel brakes are very powerful and the use of undue pressure is unnecessary. Fierce application causes undue transmission and tyre wear.
4. On icy, wet, damp, and loose road surfaces apply the brakes with special care to prevent skidding. Skidding is *always* dangerous.
5. When braking becomes essential, start braking well before you come to an obstruction, HALT sign, or a traffic signal showing amber, red, or red and amber.
6. Never brake when the motor-cycle is banked over.
7. Remember that braking takes longer to slow down the machine when you are travelling fast.
8. Brake and stop before entering a major road from a side road. Many bad accidents are caused through motor-cyclists and car drivers crossing a major road without stopping at the junction. A sign is not always provided to indicate a major road ahead.

Hints on Fuel Economy. Ariel motor-cycles are designed to run many miles per gallon of petroil mixture. Observance of the following hints will ensure maximum economy and minimum expense—
  1. Always see that the machine is tanked up with a petroil mixture having the *correct proportions* of petrol and two-stroke oil.
  2. Use premium grade petrol and a good brand of oil.
  3. Avoid continuous fast driving and excessively high engine revolutions in the lower gears.
  4. Do not allow the engine to tick-over in *neutral* for long periods.
  5. Avoid traffic jams if possible.
  6. Close the fuel tap about 200 yards before you reach your garage or a parking space. This prevents petrol evaporation in the carburettor float chamber, which increases the oil ratio. The fuel left in the float chamber will afterwards not undergo satisfactory combustion.

Proper Running-in is Vital. During the first 1,000 miles it is imperative to run-in a new or reconditioned two-stroke Ariel properly. As regards the engine, impatience during its early life can lead to engine efficiency being *permanently* spoiled. The surfaces of new parts, especially the cylinder bores, although accurately finished and apparently dead smooth, when examined under a lens are seen to have tool marks which require gentle rubbing down until the surfaces acquire a mirror-like gloss.

Excessive or unduly low engine revolutions during the running-in period cause undue friction and insufficient lubrication respectively, both of which are harmful. Always keep the engine running at a *reasonable speed* and on no account travel at a high road speed for long distances. Keep your maximum speed in any gear well down until running-in is completed. Other important running-in points to observe are as follows—

  1. Always replenish the fuel tank with a recommended and reliable type of petroil mixture having the correct petrol/oil ratio (*see* page 11).
  2. Do not use any but the types of sparking plugs recommended by Ariel Motors Ltd. For the Leader and Arrow, recommended types during *and after* running-in are the Lodge 2HLN and the Champion N3. These plugs are of the 14-mm type with ¾ in. reach.
  3. Keep the gearbox filled to the correct level and with the correct type of oil (*see* page 22).
  4. Avoid very small and big throttle openings. Make full use of the gearbox and alter the throttle opening as required to maintain proper lubrication.
  5. On a four-stroke engine it is permissible to ride down steep or long hills with top gear engaged and the throttle practically closed. On two-stroke engines, however, ride down such hills with a lower gear engaged and the throttle slightly opened.
  6. Do not interfere with the carburettor setting, especially the throttle

HANDLING YOUR MACHINE

stop (*see* page 29) which is initially adjusted to give the best tick-over speed.

7. Occasionally check for tightness the various external bolts and nuts. As bedding down occurs these are liable to slacken off slightly.

8. Under no circumstances allow the engine to "pink." Continued pinking can end in piston seizure. Pinking can be due to an unsuitable petroil mixture, unsuitable sparking plugs, an incorrect contact-breaker gap, or an excessive tightening of the front and/or rear brake adjustment.

Should you be unable to trace the reason for your engine's pinking, consult the Ariel dealer from whom you bought your machine. He will, if you wish, under the "Ariel Free Service Scheme" examine the condition of your mount after 1,000 miles running-in. Finally, during the running-in period avoid being "run in" yourself by following the sound advice given in the *Highway Code*.

CHAPTER II

CORRECT LUBRICATION

REGULAR lubrication of the engine, gearbox, and various motor-cycle components, using recommended lubricants, will maintain high performance and prevent unnecessary wear. Correct lubrication of your Ariel Leader or Arrow is quite simple, but *essential*.

The Petroil Lubrication System. All two-stroke engines, including the Ariel transverse twin engine, have a much less complex system of lubrication system than that used on four-stroke engines. There is no separate oil tank, no oil pump, no filters, and no rockers for overhead valves requiring lubrication. Inlet, transfer, and exhaust ports are automatically opened and closed during upward and downward movement of the piston in each cylinder. Each two-stroke cycle of operations, as you probably know, involves one complete upward stroke and one complete downward stroke of the piston. Maintenance as regards petroil lubrication is negligible. A brief outline of the Ariel petroil lubrication system is as follows. It applies to *each* cylinder.

The petroil (a mixture of petrol and oil) in the fuel tank, is combined with air, vaporized by, and automatically fed from, the carburettor direct into the *crankcase* of the engine during each *upward* piston stroke. When the piston is near the bottom of its subsequent *downward* stroke a *transfer port* is opened by the piston and allows vaporized and compressed petrol to pass from the crankcase into the cylinder combustion chamber which is in a state of semi-vacuum above the piston. When the engine is *hot* petrol evaporation from the petroil mixture becomes considerably more rapid and complete than when the engine is cold; hence the undesirability of kicking the engine over too often with the ignition switched off, and of allowing the engine to run too slowly when ticking-over.

Proper evaporation of the petrol from the petroil mixture and its transfer into the combustion chamber leaves *neat oil mist* to lubricate the engine bearings and piston. With the petroil system the oil mist provided to lubricate the engine is automatically measured out in proportion to the power output of the engine. The more the throttle is opened, the greater is the amount of oil mist produced. In spite of the fact that there is no oil pump, adequate lubrication of the engine is assured and is automatic.

Note the Lubrication Chart. Fig. 14 shows a lubrication chart applicable to the Ariel Leader and Arrow. It indicates the location of the main

CORRECT LUBRICATION

lubrication points. The numerals preceding the subsequent paragraphs apply to the numerals shown in the lubrication chart.

1. ALWAYS USE A CORRECT PETROIL MIXTURE. You can have a suitable petroil mixture inserted through the filler cap of the fuel tank under the dualseat, or insert, or have inserted, the two-stroke oil and premium

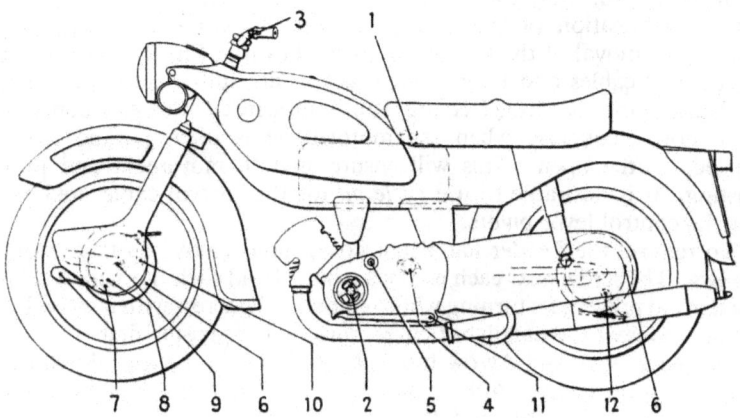

FIG. 14. LUBRICATION CHART SHOWING WHERE YOUR ARIEL LEADER OR ARROW NEEDS REGULAR ATTENTION

The numbers apply to the numbers preceding the paragraphs included in this chapter. Except where oil is stated below, grease is required, and grease nipples are provided for items 7-12.

1. Fuel tank (petroil).
2. Contact-breaker cam (oil).
3. Handlebar control cables and lever pivots (oil and grease).
4. Four-speed gearbox (oil).
5. Oilbath primary chaincase (oil).
6. Front and rear hub bearings.
7. Front anchor bar.
8. Trailing links of front forks.
9. Front-brake plate bush.
10. Front-brake cam spindle.
11. Rear-brake pedal spindle and centre stand.
12. Rear-brake cam spindle.

(*Diagram by courtesy of Ariel Motors Ltd.*)

grade petrol separately. Instructions for raising the dualseat and replenishing the fuel tank are given on pages 5 and 10 respectively.

2. CONTACT-BREAKER CAM LUBRICATION. Every 2,500 miles some slight lubrication is necessary. On a Leader first remove the near-side panel (*see* page 48). To obtain access to the contact-breaker assembly on the Leader and Arrow, remove the circular cover secured by three screws. Then apply two or three drops of *engine oil* to the felt pad provided for lubricating the cam which operates the upper contact for the near-side cylinder and the lower contact for the off-side cylinder respectively. Neglect in this matter will cause wear of the moving contact rocker-arm ends bearing on the cam. If the cam is dry you can usually hear a slight squeak if you slowly rotate the engine. Be most careful not

to add excessive engine oil to the felt pad, otherwise there is a risk of oil getting on the contacts with the result that some misfiring will develop.

3. HANDLEBAR CONTROL CABLES AND CONTROL LEVER PIVOTS. The three handlebar controls requiring regular lubrication are: the front brake lever, the clutch lever, and the throttle twist-grip. On the Leader proper lubrication of the front brake and clutch controls requires preliminary removal of the handlebar cover shown in Fig. 9. On the Arrow all control cables and lever pivot brackets are fully exposed as there is no handlebar cover fitted (*see* Fig. 10). Lubricate as often as is convenient, and more frequently when the motor-cycle is often parked for long periods in the open. This will ensure smooth movement and prevent rusting. It is desirable to use *cycle oil* for the control cables and *grease* for the control lever pivots.

To remove the Leader handlebar cover, first remove its *three* securing screws. The screw near each end has a nut. Hold each nut with a suitable spanner to prevent its turning while removing the screw with a screwdriver. Then withdraw the handlebar cover, raising its near side first.

On the Leader and Arrow lubricate the front brake and clutch cables and pivots as follows. Pull and hold each lever inwards, thereby exposing the inner control cable and the bracket used as a pivot for the lever. Lightly *grease* the bracket where the control lever pivots, and add a few drops of *cycle oil* to the nipple on the handlebar lever and also to the exposed portion of the inner cable.

In the case of the throttle twist-grip fitted to the Leader and Arrow, add a few drops of *cycle oil* to lubricate the inner cable, controlled by the throttle twist-grip, after turning the twist-grip *fully inwards*, closing it and simultaneously pulling the outer cable away from the twist-grip. Be most careful not to lose the split bush located between the twist-grip and the outer control cable. It is desirable after a considerable mileage has been covered to remove all three cables from the handlebar controls and oil the cables thoroughly by injecting oil throughout their length.

When replacing the handlebar cover on a Leader, see that the nylon spacers are in sound condition, and located properly in the clutch and front-brake lever brackets. Also when tightening down the cover by means of the three securing screws, make sure that each of the two end screws has its chromium plated washer fitted beneath its head and that the securing screw is pushed through the cover and nylon spacer *before* replacing the washer and nut below. Tighten each nut firmly but not excessively.

4. THE FOUR-SPEED GEARBOX. The teeth are subjected to immense stresses and correct lubrication is *essential*. The capacity of the gearbox is *one pint* and lubricants recommended for summer and winter use are: Castrol XL, Mobiloil A, Essolube 30, B.P. Energol 30, or Shell X100-30. Check the oil level regularly, weekly if practicable, and top-up with

CORRECT LUBRICATION

suitable grade S.A.E. 30 oil to the *correct level*. Drain, flush, and refill the gearbox with suitable oil to the correct level every 5,000 miles.

To top-up or drain and refill the gearbox on a Leader it is necessary first to remove the off-side panel (*see* page 48), and on an Arrow the engine cover on the same side (*see* page 49) can be removed to expose the gearbox for draining and replenishment.

To check that there is sufficient oil in the gearbox, remove the level screw whose position is marked on the offside of the gearbox casing. Oil should then just trickle out. If it does not do so and the oil level is clearly low, top-up the gearbox on a Leader as follows. First take off the clutch-adjuster cover in the centre of the gearbox casing after removing the two securing screws. Then top-up with recommended oil by pouring it (using a small funnel if necessary) through the large hole until it just begins to trickle from the oil-level screw hole. Afterwards replace and firmly tighten the oil-level screw with its fibre washer attached. Finally replace the clutch-adjuster cover and its joint washer. Never top-up the gearbox without first removing the oil level screw, otherwise excessive oil may be added, causing difficult gear changing and other trouble.

To top-up the gearbox on an Arrow removal of the engine cover is *not* essential. Remove the large rubber grummet fitted in the side of the engine cover. This gives access to the oil-level screw. Then inject suitable oil with an oilcan of the pump type through the hole for the screw until it begins to trickle out. To facilitate replacement of the level-plug screw, grease the end of the screwdriver.

To drain and refill the gearbox, unscrew and remove the drain plug which is below the oil-level screw. The position of the drain plug is also marked. Then with the *oil warm* allow the whole of the oil to drain from the gearbox into a convenient receptacle. Afterwards pour about 1 pint of oil through the hole exposed by removal of the clutch-adjuster cover until oil begins to trickle out from the hole exposed by removal of the oil-level screw. Finally replace and firmly tighten both screws, with fibre washers attached, and replace the clutch-adjuster cover and its joint washer. As previously mentioned in the paragraph about topping-up, *on no account fill the gearbox with excessive oil*.

After topping-up or refilling the gearbox, replace the side panel or engine cover in the case of a Leader or Arrow respectively.

5. THE OILBATH PRIMARY CHAINCASE. Some oil from the primary chaincase (capacity $1\frac{3}{4}$ pint) is automatically fed (*see* Fig. 16) to the secondary chain, and therefore the level of oil in the primary chaincase gradually falls. Every 1,000 miles check the oil level and top-up if necessary. Drain, flush, and refill the chaincase every 5,000 miles. Recommended grade S.A.E. 20 oils for summer and winter use are: Wakefield Castrolite, Mobiloil Arctic, Esso Extra Motor Oil 20W30, B.P. Energol 20W, or Shell X100 20/20W.

To check the oil level in the primary chaincase, or to drain and refill the case it is, of course, necessary on a Leader first to remove the near-side panel (*see* page 48). Then, referring to Fig. 15, remove the oil-level plug 1. Oil should just trickle out from the plug hole. If it does not do so and the level is low, top-up the chaincase with one of the previously mentioned oils, otherwise rapid chain wear is likely to occur. Remove the large chain-tension inspection cap 2 and pour oil through the hole until oil does begin to trickle out from the oil-level plug hole. It is desirable when topping-up the chaincase to check the tension of the primary chain

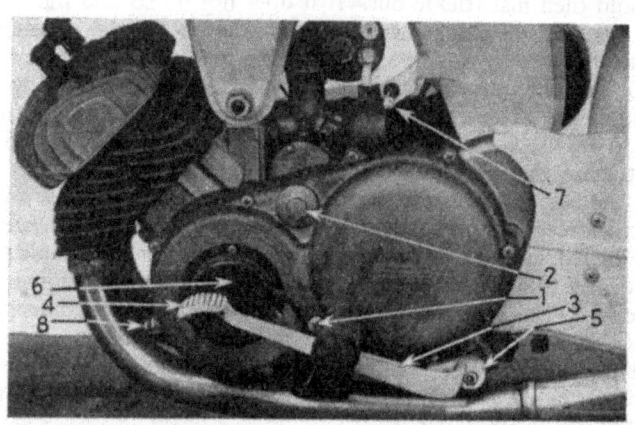

FIG. 15. NEAR-SIDE VIEW OF POWER UNIT SHOWING OILBATH PRIMARY CHAINCASE AND OTHER DETAILS

1. Oil level plug.
2. Inspection cap (for chain tension and oilbath replenishment).
3. Location of oilbath drain plug.
4. Rear brake pedal.
5. Pinch-bolt and nut securing rear brake lever to serrated shaft.
6. Contact-breaker cover.
7. Cold-starting control knob.
8. Chain tension adjuster.

(*see* page 62). Afterwards replace and firmly tighten the oil-level plug and the inspection cap, not omitting to replace the attached washers.

Drain and refill the oilbath primary chaincase as follows. Referring to Fig. 15, drain off the oil when *warm* into a suitable receptacle by removing the drain plug. Its position, indicated at 3, is on the chaincase below its rear circular portion covering the clutch. To obtain access to the drain plug it is necessary to remove the lever of the rear brake pedal 4 from its serrated shaft after slackening the pinch-bolt and removing the nut 5. After allowing *all* oil to drain off, replace and firmly tighten the drain plug and insert about ¾ pint of suitable oil through the inspection cap hole until the oil begins to trickle out from the oil-level plug hole. Afterwards replace the level plug, the inspection cap, and the rear-brake pedal lever. Position the lever on its shaft correctly (*see* page 66). Finally on the Leader replace the near-side panel.

CORRECT LUBRICATION 25

6. THE FRONT AND REAR HUBS. The full-width hub of the front wheel and the wheel and sprocket assembly of the rear wheel both have two journal type non-adjustable ball bearings. During initial assembly at the Ariel factory these bearings are well packed with *grease*. This suffices until the speedometer mileage recorder registers 5,000 miles. Then, and subsequently every 5,000 miles, remove each wheel, remove the old grease, clean, and pack the bearings with fresh grease of the recommended

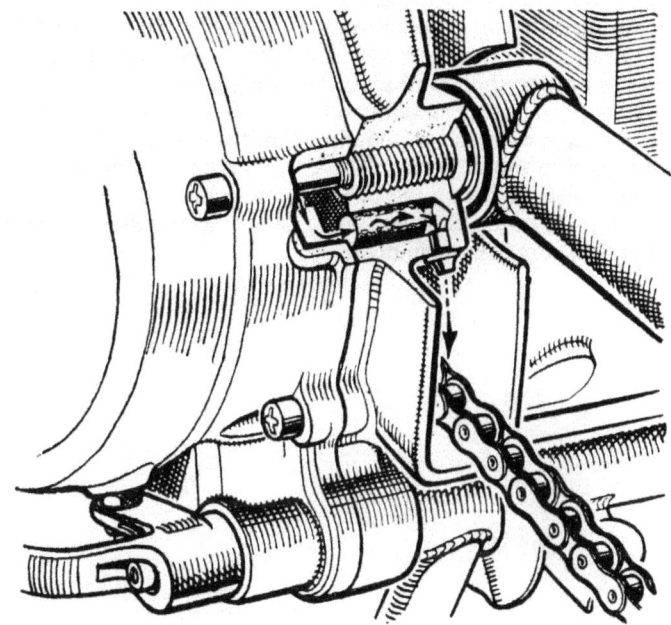

FIG. 16. SECTIONAL VIEW SHOWING HOW THE SECONDARY CHAIN IS AUTOMATICALLY LUBRICATED

A felt wick and zerk plug in the rear half of the oilbath primary chaincase feeds oil to the lower run of the secondary chain. Should the zerk plug become choked, clear it with a piece of wire. The felt wick is renewable if necessary. Note the brake pedal height adjustment below the rear of the chain case.

(*By courtesy of "Motor Cycle," London*)

type. Note that *no grease nipples* are provided for lubricating the hub bearings.

Recommended greases to use for the front and rear hub bearings and all other grease points on a Leader or Arrow motor-cycle are: Wakefield Castrolease LM, Mobilgrease MP, B.P. Energrease L2, or Esso Multi-purpose grease H.

7. THE FRONT ANCHOR BAR. Every 5,000 miles apply some grease with a grease gun to the *two* nipples provided for lubrication.

8. THE FRONT FORKS. No lubrication is necessary other than to inject some grease (2-3 strokes) about every 1,000 miles through the nipple provided on the light-alloy trailing link fitted to each front fork leg.

9. THE FRONT-BRAKE PLATE BUSH. A grease nipple is provided at the end of the front wheel spindle for lubricating the floating brake plate bush. Every 1,000 miles inject some grease sparingly through the nipple. Avoid excessive greasing.

10. THE FRONT-BRAKE CAM SPINDLE. Every 1,000 miles inject with the grease gun (one stroke) grease through the nipple fitted to the brake cam spindle bearing. Do not over grease, otherwise some of it may get on the linings of the brake shoes and reduce braking power.

11. THE REAR-BRAKE PEDAL SPINDLE AND CENTRE STAND. Every 1,000 miles apply the grease gun to the nipple on the brake pedal lever. A fair amount of grease should be injected as it lubricates the brake cross shaft (the spindle) and also the pivot of the centre stand.

12. THE REAR-BRAKE CAM SPINDLE. Grease as described in paragraph 10 for the front-brake cam spindle.

CHAPTER III

THE AMAL CARBURETTOR

AN Amal "Monobloc" type No. 375/33 carburettor is fitted to the engine of all Ariel Leader and Arrow motor-cycles. On the Sports Arrow the engine has a similar carburettor, type No. 376/277, with a different size main jet. The carburettor settings recommended by the makers and provided on new machines should rarely be interfered with as they ensure good performance and economy. These settings are given on page 28. If the engine runs well at all speeds with the engine in sound mechanical condition, correctly lubricated, and not in need of decarbonizing, leave the carburettor alone. Occasionally it may be necessary to make an adjustment to improve slow-running and tick-over (*see* page 29). Every 5,000 miles remove any foreign matter collected in the float-chamber or main jet cover nut. After a very considerable mileage has been covered remove, dismantle, inspect, and thoroughly clean the carburettor. Apart from this, no maintenance is normally required.

All Amal carburettors fitted to Ariel 247 c.c. two-stroke engines have an air filter (with renewable element) fitted externally. This ensures that *clean* air always enters the carburettor through its air intake. The elimination of dust keeps the carburettor clean and reduces engine wear.

The Carburettor Controls. Only *two* controls are provided: the throttle twist-grip on the handlebars and the knob for actuating the cold-starting device. The use of the latter has been previously referred to on page 13. After starting the engine and pushing the knob right home, engine speed is entirely controlled by the throttle twist-grip.

The cold-starting device includes a butterfly choke and adaptor clamped to the air-intake of the carburettor. This "strangler" ensures very rapid starting from cold and eliminates the need for wasteful "flooding" of the carburettor by means of the tickler shown at 7 in Fig. 18, in the case of an Arrow or Sports Arrow with no side panel. The instrument has no air valve as fitted on carburettors used on the majority of four-stroke motorcycles and shown at 3 in Fig. 18.

How the Carburettor Works. Summing-up, it mixes in the correct proportions and vaporizes the petroil (gravity fed from the fuel tank into the float chamber) with air sucked through the air filter attached to the "strangler" adaptor. The vaporized mixture of petroil and air is sucked into the engine crankcase during each upward piston stroke and transferred through the transfer port into each cylinder where it is compressed by the piston and fired by the sparking plug.

Dealing with the "Monobloc" carburettor in more detail, and referring to Fig. 18, the float chamber (13) and nylon float needle (9) maintain a constant level of petrol in the needle jet (14) and the pilot jet (17). The selection by the makers of the appropriate jet sizes and choke size ensures a proper atomizing and proportioning of the petrol and air sucked into the engine.

The carburettor works in four stages. When opening the throttle from the fully closed position to one-eighth open (for tick-over) the mixture is supplied by the pilot jet (17), and the strength of the mixture is decided by the setting of the knurled pilot air-adjusting screw (20) which has a coil locking-spring. As the throttle is slightly opened farther, the main jet system comes into action, the mixture being augmented by the main jet (16) through the pilot jet by-pass.

The amount of cut-away on the atmospheric side of the throttle valve regulates the petroil-to-air ratio between one-eighth and one-quarter throttle. The needle jet (14) and the jet needle (23) take over the regulation of the mixture between one-quarter and three-quarter throttle, and the mixture strength is determined by the relative position of the needle in the clip (4) attached to the throttle valve (24). When the throttle is opened beyond three-quarters, the mixture strength is determined only by the size of the main jet. Note that the main jet does not spray petrol direct into the carburettor mixing chamber, but discharges through the needle jet (14) into the primary air chamber. An angled spray tube is fitted on carburettors having a size 140 main jet, but not on those with a size 170 jet (applicable to Leader engines with engine No. prior to T7921). From the primary chamber the petrol vapour enters the air main choke through the primary air choke. The latter has a two-way compensating action in conjunction with the "bleed" holes in the needle jet. Pilot and main jet behaviour are not affected by this two-way compensation which controls only acceleration at normal cruising speed.

Leader and Arrow Carburettor Settings. For the 1958–66 models with Amal type No. 375/33 "Monobloc" carburettor the correct setting is: throttle valve $3\frac{3}{4}$; main jet, size 140; pilot jet, size 30; needle jet, 0·105; needle position, 3.

A main jet size 170 is correct for earlier Leader carburettors not fitted with an angled spray tube.

Sports Arrow Settings. For the 1960–6 Sports Arrow the correct settings for the Amal type No. 376/277 "Monobloc" carburettor is as stated above for the No. 375/33 carburettor, except that a size 230 main jet is required. The needle position 3 is normally recommended for the specially tuned engine, but on certain engines if the mixture shows signs of weakness or richness, with the carburettor correctly adjusted, it may be desirable to raise or lower the needle position *one notch* respectively. After altering the needle position the slow-running adjustment must be altered to suit.

Throttle Cable Adjustment. An adjuster for the throttle valve cable is provided (*see* Fig. 17) on top of the mixing chamber cap. Keep this adjusted so that as you begin to turn the throttle twist-grip inwards some very slight slackness in the cable is present. To make an adjustment, screw the adjuster in or out as required.

Altering Slow-running Adjustment. An adjustment should be made if the engine ticks over too slowly with the throttle twist-grip in the closed position. A two-stroke engine, unlike a four-stroke type, requires a fairly fast tick-over to ensure proper lubrication of the engine. A throttle-stop adjusting screw (*see* Fig. 17) is fitted to position the throttle valve or slide so that it keeps the engine ticking over when the throttle twist-grip is in the fully closed position. An adjustment is also necessary if the slow-running mixture is too weak or rich. Too weak a mixture is indicated by a tendency for the mixture to spit back, poor acceleration, overheating, and by power lag when the throttle is snapped open. Too rich a mixture causes four-stroking and a smoky exhaust to occur. Both are bad for the engine and annoying to the rider when allowing the engine to idle with *neutral* engaged and while riding with a small throttle opening. Smooth tick-over and slow running are dependent on the setting of the pilot air-adjusting screw (*see* Fig. 17) which controls the mixture strength up to one-eighth throttle opening, irrespective of the pilot jet size.

The normal adjustment of the pilot air-adjusting screw is $2\frac{1}{2}$ *complete turns outwards*. A combined adjustment of the throttle-stop adjusting screw and the pilot air-adjusting screw is usually necessary to obtain a smooth idling speed. This adjustment should be made as described in the following paragraph.

On a Leader first remove the off-side panel to obtain acess to the car-burettor adjuster screws. Start up the engine, close the "strangler," and warm it up to its normal running temperature. Then *screw in* the pilot air-adjusting screw until the mixture is excessively rich and the engine begins to run unevenly. When this happens weaken the mixture by *unscrewing* the pilot air-adjusting screw until the engine runs evenly with the throttle twist-grip closed. With the pilot air-adjusting screw properly adjusted it may be found that the engine is running too fast. In this case *unscrew* the throttle-stop adjusting screw until the engine runs at a moderate speed. Where a considerable adjustment of the throttle-stop adjusting screw has to be made to regulate engine speed, further adjustment of the pilot air-adjustment screw may be necessary to obtain a perfect slow-running mixture. Note that weakening the mixture will not improve fuel

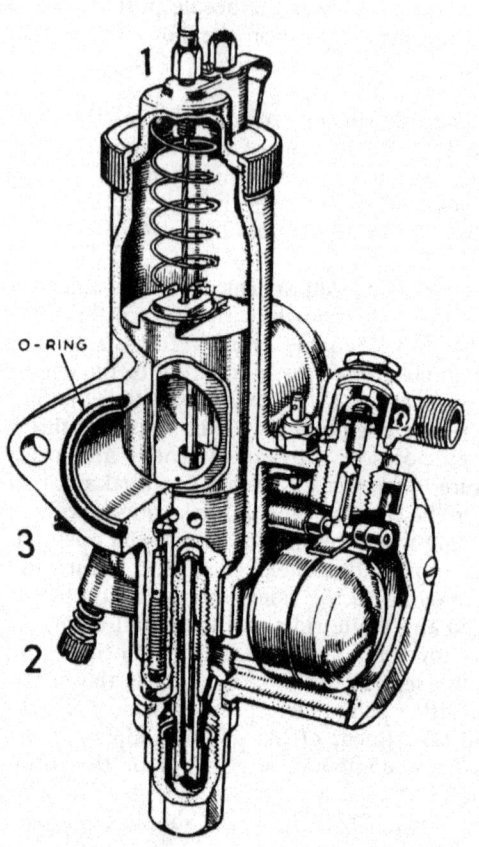

FIG. 17. SECTIONAL VIEW OF AMAL "MONOBLOC" CARBURETTOR SHOWING THE THREE ADJUSTER SCREWS

An exploded view of the carburettor is shown in Fig. 18. The O-ring (not shown in Fig. 18) reduces the risk of air leaks caused through slight flange distortion which sometimes occurs. A small gauze filter (not shown in Fig. 18) is located below the fuel pipe banjo. A butterfly type "strangler" in the air intake replaces the air valve shown at (3) in Fig. 18.

1. Throttle-cable adjuster screw.   2. Pilot air-adjusting screw.
3. Throttle-stop adjusting screw.

(*By courtesy of "Motor Cycle," London*)

consumption and is most undesirable. Note also that an excessively rich mixture besides causing four-stroking will cause excessive running on the pilot jet while riding and thus an increase in fuel consumption. Do not interfere with the carburettor settings (*see* page 28).

To Remove the Carburettor. Removal of the Amal "Monobloc" carburettor (necessary only after a very big mileage has been covered) in order to dismantle, clean, and inspect its components, should be done as follows.

On a Leader remove *both* side panels (*see* page 48). On an Arrow or Sports Arrow, remove the Lucas electric horn. Next disconnect at the carburettor end the rubber connector between the rear engine bracket and the cold starting device adaptor clamped to the air-intake of the carburettor. Loosen the clamp bolt on the off side of the adaptor clamp, and turn the adaptor *anticlockwise*. The rod operating the cold-starting device can then be slipped out of the lever on the adaptor and withdrawn.

Now, with the fuel tap closed, undo the union nut from the upper end of the fuel pipe. Also free the throttle cable from the carburettor by fully unscrewing (anticlockwise) the mixing-chamber cap ring while pressing down on the mixing-chamber cap (*see* Fig. 18). Then withdraw from the carburettor simultaneously the cap (with throttle cable attached), the throttle valve, and the jet needle. Tie up the assembly in a safe position out of the way to prevent damage. Finally, to remove the remainder of the carburettor as a unit from the engine lug above the crankcase, remove the two securing nuts and washers and pull the unit to the rear. Be careful not to damage or loose the O-ring fitted to the carburettor flange (*see* Fig. 17).

Dismantling the Carburettor. The upper end of the fuel pipe has already been disconnected from the fuel tank during the removal of the carburettor. To disconnect the lower end of the pipe and completely dismantle the carburettor, use the following procedure.

Referring to Fig. 18, remove the banjo bolt (8) which secures the fuel pipe to the top of the float chamber (13). Be careful not to lose or damage the nylon gauze filter which is exposed and can be withdrawn. To obtain access to the float (10), remove the three screws (11) and remove the float-chamber cover (12), together with its washer. Lift out the hinged float (10) and withdraw the moulded-nylon needle (9). Lay both aside for cleaning. Be careful not to lose the small spacer tube. To remove the tickler assembly (7), remove its upper nut and withdraw the tickler and spring. To remove the throttle-stop adjusting screw (18) and the pilot air-adjusting screw (20) unscrew both screws fully with a screwdriver, and withdraw. Be careful not to lose the spring attached to each screw. To remove the main jet (16), remove its cover nut from the bottom of the mixing chamber and unscrew the jet from its holder (15). Be careful not

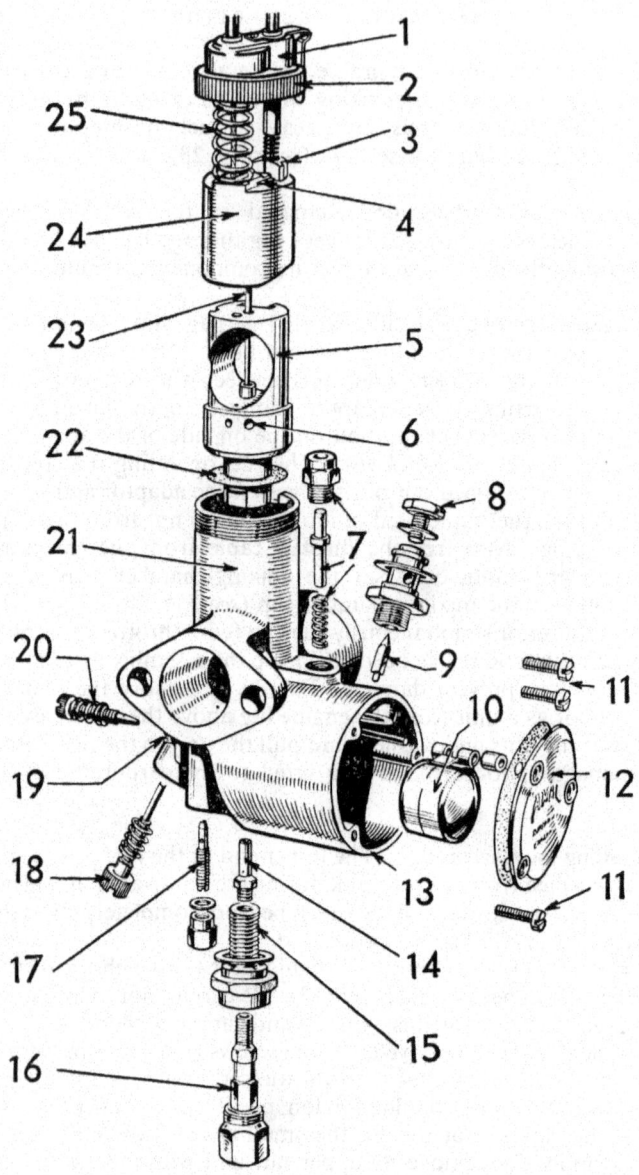

FIG. 18. EXPLODED VIEW OF AMAL "MONOBLOC" TYPE CARBURETTOR
(*See also* Fig. 17)
(*See page 33 for Key*)

to lose the washer on the main-jet holder. To remove the needle jet (14) unscrew it from the top of the main-jet holder after unscrewing the latter. Use the same spanner as used for removing the main jet to remove the needle jet. To remove the pilot jet (17), remove its cover nut and washer, and unscrew the jet with a screwdriver from the mixing chamber. Finally to remove the jet block (5), remove the jet-block locating screw (19) which is to the left of and slightly below the pilot air-adjusting screw (20). Then push or tap out the jet block (5) from the mixing chamber (21). Be careful not to lose the fibre seal (22). This completes dismantling, but if it is desired to remove the jet needle (23) from the throttle valve (24), withdraw the jet needle clip (4) and pull the needle out downwards.

Removal of the Cold-starting Unit. This has not been mentioned in the previous paragraph because its complete removal is normally unnecessary. To ensure no air leaks, the joint between the butterfly adaptor and air intake is a tight fit. As previously mentioned, removal of the carburettor requires slackening of the adaptor clamp-bolt and turning the adaptor anticlockwise in order to disconnect the cold-starting operating rod. Should it be necessary for some reason to remove the butterfly adaptor, pull the unit firmly and carefully to the rear.

Cleaning the Carburettor. Wash all the components thoroughly clean with petrol or paraffin, preferably petrol, and blow through the various ducts and passages to make certain that they are quite clear. Pay special attention to the small pilot jet passages in the jet block (5), and see that all impurities are removed from the inside of the float chamber (13). See also that the main and pilot jets are quite clean, and on no account poke a wire through them. Blow them clear if obstructed. Also clean thoroughly the gauze filter below the banjo securing bolt (8). When cleaning the carburettor components *never use a fluffy rag*.

Inspecting Carburettor Components. After dismantling and thoroughly cleaning the components it is wise if a very big mileage has been covered to inspect carefully the various parts for signs of wear or damage.

(Key to Fig. 18)

1. Mixing-chamber cap.
2. Mixing-chamber cap ring.
3. Air valve (omitted on Ariels).
4. Jet-needle clip.
5. Jet block.
6. Air passage to pilot jet.
7. Tickler assembly.
8. Banjo securing bolt.
9. Float needle.
10. Float.
11. Float-chamber cover screws.
12. Float-chamber cover.
13. Float chamber.
14. Needle jet.
15. Main-jet holder.
16. Main jet and cover nut.
17. Pilot jet.
18. Throttle-stop adjusting screw.
19. Jet-block locating screw.
20. Pilot air-adjusting screw.
21. Mixing chamber.
22. Fibre seal.
23. Jet needle.
24. Throttle valve.
25. Throttle-valve return spring.

1. THE FLOAT CHAMBER. See that the float-chamber vent, included in the tickler assembly (7) is not obstructed, and that the float is in perfect condition and the float chamber absolutely clean. If the gauze filter below the banjo securing bolt (8) is not in perfect condition, renew it. Clean the nylon float needle (9) with the greatest care and renew this also if damaged.

2. THE THROTTLE VALVE. Test the throttle valve (24) for fit in the mixing chamber (21) and renew the slide if excessive play is detected. When renewing the throttle valve, make sure that it is of the correct type (*see* page 28) with the correct amount of cut-away. This is most important.

3. THE JET-NEEDLE CLIP. Check that the spring clip (4) securing the tapered needle to the throttle valve (24) grips the needle *firmly*. Free rotation must not occur. Always be sure that the needle is replaced with the clip in the correct groove (No. 3 from the top).

4. THE CARBURETTOR FLANGE. Slight distortion of the flange sometimes occurs through excessive and uneven tightening of the flange securing nuts. This can cause an air leak where an O-ring (*see* Fig. 17) is not fitted. If the rubber sealing ring which is fitted in a recess in the joint flange is in good condition, do not remove it. Fit a new sealing ring if the old one is perished or damaged. Prise out the old ring with the blade of screwdriver and press the new ring in by hand.

5. SPECIAL COMPOSITION WASHER. Examine the condition of the special composition washer which fits over the carburettor studs between the carburettor flange and the engine lug. If in any way damaged, renew this washer which is made of an insulating material which prevents the engine heating up the carburettor.

Assembling the Carburettor. Referring to Fig. 18, screw home the pilot jet (17), followed by the fibre washer and the pilot-jet cover nut. Replace the pilot air-adjusting screw (20) and the throttle-stop air-adjusting screw (18), and tighten the screws until the springs are slightly compressed. Push or tap home the jet block (5) and the fibre seal (22) into the mixing chamber (21). Check that the fibre seal is in good condition. When the jet block is right home, fit and tighten securely the jet block locating-screw (19). Now screw the main-jet holder (15) into the jet block, after checking that the washer for the holder is sound. Then screw the main jet and cover nut (16) into the main-jet holder. Tighten both securely.

Dealing with the float chamber, replace the tickler assembly (7) and tighten the external nut securely. The tickler should, of course, protrude from the nut. Next fit the union on the lower part of the fuel pipe to the top of the float chamber and tighten the large nut securely. Replace the larger washer and above it the nylon filter, with the flange of the filter *downward*. Fit the fuel-pipe banjo union over the nylon filter and replace the banjo securing bolt and washer (8). Tighten the nut lightly. Now insert the moulded-nylon needle (9) through the float chamber (13) into the lower end of the fuel pipe union, so that only the round short end of the nylon needle projects into the float chamber. Position the hinged float (10) in the float chamber so that the centre of the hinged portion forms a platform to support the nylon needle. Fit the short spacer tube to the end of the float hinge and replace the float-chamber cover (12). If the washer is not in perfect condition, renew it. Firmly but evenly tighten the three screws (11) which secure the cover.

If previously removed, attach the jet needle (23) to the throttle valve (24) and secure with the jet-needle clip (4). Be sure that the clip enters the correct groove (*see* page 28).

To Replace the Carburettor. Before replacing the carburettor on the engine, thoroughly clean the face of the engine lug and clean and inspect the special composition washer fitted to the lug. It must be in perfect condition. Then fit the carburettor flange over the two studs projecting from the engine lug, and replace the two shake-proof washers and the carburettor securing nuts. It is most important to tighten both nuts evenly a little at a time, otherwise the carburettor flange may become distorted and cause trouble.

Replace the throttle valve (24) in the mixing chamber (21) with the cut-away at the bottom of the slide facing to the *rear*. When easing the throttle valve home, see that the tapered jet needle (23) enters the holes in the jet block (5) and exert no pressure until the jet needle is properly positioned. As the throttle valve goes right home, position the mixing-chamber cap (1) on the top of the mixing chamber so that the locating peg on the under side of the cap engages the slot in the top edge of the mixing chamber. Then tighten down firmly the knurled cap ring (2) and check that the throttle valve slides smoothly when operating the twist-grip. Assembly is now complete except for connecting the operating rod of the cold-starting device, and air filter rubber, and the fuel pipe.

Reconnecting the Operating Rod of the Cold-starting Device. Fit the operating rod into the frame bracket, and then slip the cranked end of the rod through the small hole in the end of the lever on the adaptor clamped to the carburettor air-intake. It is assumed that the adaptor is in the same position as was necessary for removal of the rod (*see* page 31). Now turn the adaptor *clockwise* until the lever is uppermost and horizontal. Afterwards firmly tighten the adaptor clamp bolt on the off side.

Final Assembly. Reconnect the rubber from the air filter to the adaptor on the air-intake. Moisten the end of the connector rubber with petrol or petroil on the inside and push the end of the rubber connector over the end of the adaptor. It should push over easily. Do not twist the rubber connector when attaching it. Reconnect the upper end of the fuel pipe to the fuel tap and tighten the union nut securely. Also firmly tighten the banjo bolt (8) on the float-chamber union. Start up the engine and make the necessary slow-running adjustment. Finally, when satisfied with the adjustment, on a Leader replace both side panels. On an Arrow replace the Lucas electric horn. As far as carburation is concerned, everything should now be in order, assuming you have not been careless during assembly and carburettor adjustment.

The Air Filter. Except where riding frequently on extremely dusty roads it is not necessary to renew the filter element more often than about every 10,000 miles. The filter ensures clean air being admitted to the carburettor via an induction silencer formed in the frame of the motor-cycle for the purpose of eliminating air-intake noise. It is fitted on the off side to a short tube on the rear frame to engine bracket. Renewal of the filter element should be effected as follows.

On a Leader remove the side panel (*see* page 48) from the off side of the machine. Then pull the filter assembly firmly outwards to remove it. Lightly compress the perforated cover and lift out the fixing clip. Then withdraw the dirty element, wipe the cover and end plates absolutely clean. Fit a new element, replace the perforated cover, compress it, and secure it with the fixing clip. An alternative to renewing the filter element is to wash the dirty element very thoroughly with clean petrol. Renewal at 10,000 mile intervals is, however, desirable because a restricted air flow reduces engine performance, and is not good for a two-stroke engine.

CHAPTER IV

THE LUCAS LIGHTING SYSTEM

ALL Ariel motor-cycles fitted with 247 c.c. parallel twin two-stroke engines have a Lucas A.C. lighting-ignition system. This includes an alternator driven by an extension of the crankshaft, and a rectifier for converting the alternating (a.c.) current supplied by the alternator to uni-directional (d.c.) current for charging the battery.

From the battery d.c. current is taken direct to the lamps when the lighting switch is switched on. Current from the battery is also taken, when the separate ignition switch is switched on, from the battery to the sparking plugs via the two separate ignition coils and the contact-breaker which has two pairs of contacts. The ignition switch has an EMG (emergency) position to facilitate starting from cold (*see* page 13) in the event of the battery being discharged.

This chapter deals with three items concerned with lighting *and* ignition (i.e. the alternator, rectifier, and battery) and with lamps, but not with items concerned solely with the ignition system, i.e. the ignition coils, contact-breaker, and sparking plugs. These items are dealt with in the ignition section of Chapter V.

THE ALTERNATOR AND RECTIFIER

The Type RM 13/15 Alternator. The alternator comprises a stationary spigot-mounted 6-coil laminated stator secured to the offside of the crankcase, and a rotor which incorporates magnets and is bolted and keyed to an extension of the flywheel assembly off-side main-shaft. The alternator unit is accessible on removing the off-side panel or engine cover on a Leader or Arrow respectively, and then removing the alternator cover which is secured by three small screws. Its removal is, however, rarely necessary, as *no maintenance is normally required*. The alternator automatically keeps the battery fully charged under ordinary running conditions. Always keep the three snap connectors in the output cables (*see* Fig. 19) clean and tight; also see that the cables do not become frayed. In the unlikely event of alternator trouble occurring, have the alternator inspected and attended to by the Ariel or Lucas Service Agent. Do not meddle with the alternator yourself. The alternator is secured to the off-side main-shaft by a key and locking-nut. The removal of the nut can be effected with a box spanner and tommy-bar.

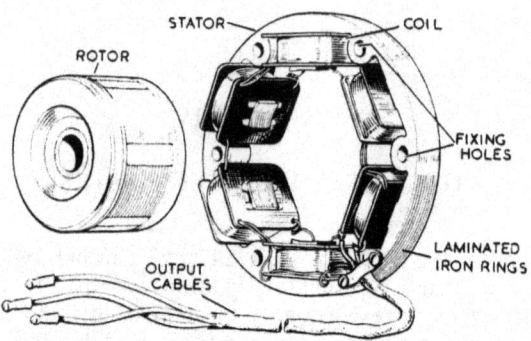

Fig. 19. Showing Stator and Rotor of the Lucas Type RM/13 Alternator

The Lucas RM 13/15 alternator fitted to the Leader and Arrow has a somewhat larger rotor and a few minor differences.

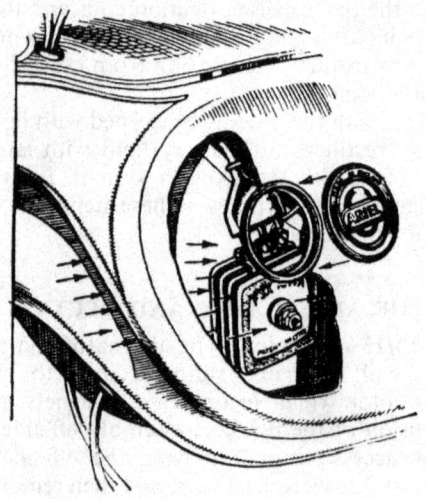

Fig. 20. On the Ariel Arrow to Obtain Access to the Rectifier, Remove the Ariel Badge as Shown

(*By courtesy of "Motor Cycle," London*)

The Rectifier. The Lucas four-plate rectifier is secured to the frame just below the steering head on the Leader and just inside the forward end of of the "dummy" tank on the Arrow, as shown in Fig. 20. It operates like a non-return valve and allows current to pass in one direction only to the battery. It is, of course, connected by cables to the alternator stator and to the battery.

No adjustment is necessary, but keep the rectifier dry and clean. It is convenient to use a small brush to remove any dirt or dust from the plates. Keep the cable connectors tight and see that the sheath provided for protecting the rubber cables is properly positioned. A separate nut is used to secure the rectifier to the frame. This must always be kept securely tightened. On no account slacken the nut which clamps the rectifier plates together at a certain pressure to ensure correct rectifier performance. Also be careful not to connect the rectifier cables incorrectly.

CARE OF THE BATTERY

The battery fitted to Leader and Arrow motor-cycles is a Lucas 13-amp, 6-volt, type ML9E, and it is of the utmost importance to keep it in good condition by regular maintenance. This is particularly important with the ML9E battery which has a smaller fluid capacity than some other types of Lucas batteries. The following are the most important maintenance hints—

1. Check the level of the electrolyte in the battery *weekly*, and if necessary top-up with distilled water to the correct level.

2. Keep the battery and terminals clean, and the terminals tight.

3. See that the battery earth lead is always connected to the *positive terminal* of the battery.

4. If your motor-cycle is to be out of service for a considerable period, fully charge the battery, remove it, and have it charged at fortnightly intervals.

Topping-up the Battery Cells. The battery is mounted under the dualseat (*see* Fig. 8) and the level of the electrolyte in each of the three cells should be checked *weekly*. To do this, raise the dualseat and lift the battery from its carrier sufficiently to observe the level of the electrolyte in each cell. Removal of the battery is not necessary. The electrolyte level can be observed through the semi-transparent plastic case. Top-up with distilled water if the electrolyte level is below the coloured line (*see* Fig. 21) marked "maximum acid level" on the battery case. If topping-up is necessary, top-up as follows.

It is preferable to top-up *before* a run, as the agitation accompanying charging and "gassing" thoroughly mixes the electrolyte solution. Remove the three filler plugs from the top of the battery after removing the battery cover. Then with a syringe insert distilled water through each filler plug hole until the electrolyte level is as indicated in Fig. 21. Distilled water is obtainable from most chemists and garages. Never top-up above the coloured line indicating the maximum filling level, and note that a Lucas battery filler is unsuitable for topping-up a Lucas type ML9E battery. Before replacing each filler plug, make sure that its vent hole is clear and the rubber sealing ring in sound condition. Tighten all three filler plugs securely. Finally replace the battery cover after wiping the top of the battery dry, position the battery, and lower the dualseat. A sponge rubber pad on the base of the dualseat keeps the battery cover in position and protects it from vibration.

Battery Terminal Connexions. To prevent corrosion it is a good plan to lightly coat them with some petroleum jelly. Always keep the connexions clean and tight. The external terminals are clearly marked to indicate which is the positive (+) and which is the negative (−) terminal. The *positive* terminal must always have its cable *earthed* to the bolt on the

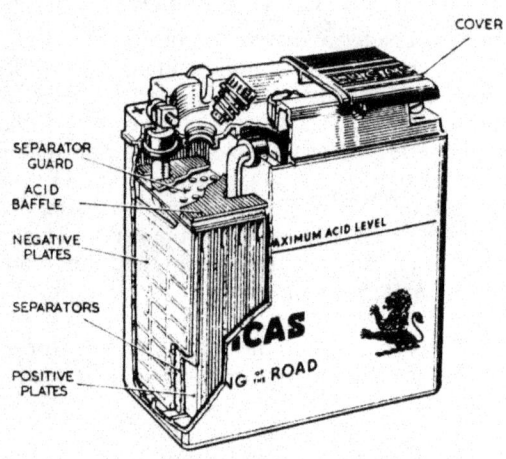

Fig. 21. The Lucas Model ML9E Battery

frame of the machine. Wrong connexion can damage the rectifier and alternator. The negative terminal connects to the main harness lead. To disconnect either terminal in order to remove the battery, remove the bolt, shake-proof washer and nut, from the terminal. The lead can then be withdrawn. Be careful not to lose the washer, and when the lead is reconnected, see that the nut is firmly tightened.

THE LAMPS

The Lucas Headlamp (Leader). This headlamp (type MCF 575P), which has a 6-in. diameter lens, and light-unit with a pre-focus double-filament main bulb and a parking bulb, is housed in a neat cowl. An unusual feature is the beam trimmer (shown at (6) in Fig. 9) on the instrument panel. This is additional to the handlebar dipper switch shown at 11 in the same illustration.

Adjust the beam trimmer to suit the load carried (i.e., with the machine off its centre stand, and seated on the dualseat with or without a pillion passenger). The beam should project straight ahead and its centre should be parallel with the road surface. A good test should be made by shining the lamp on a blank wall at a distance of about 25 ft. While riding do not use the beam trimmer.

To remove the light-unit and rim from the headlamp body to obtain access to the bulb holders, first turn the handlebars over to full lock. Then loosen the securing screw at the bottom of the rim. The rim with attached light-unit can then be removed by pulling the rim forward at its bottom end. The wiring for the main and parking bulbs will, of course, remain attached to the bulb holders.

The pre-focus double-filament main bulb has a bayonet-fixing adaptor

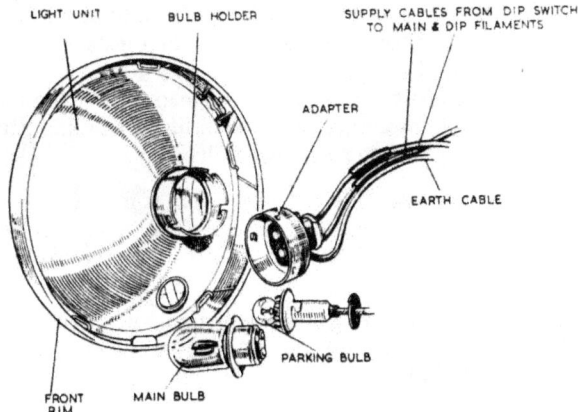

FIG. 22. LIGHT UNIT AND RIM REMOVED FROM LUCAS HEADLAMP
On the Leader a wider rim is fitted and this has a securing screw at its base.

(see Fig. 22). To remove the bulb, push the adaptor inwards, turn *anti-clockwise*, pull the adaptor off, and remove the bulb from its holder in the rear of the reflector.

If a new main bulb is required, fit a Lucas No. 166 6-volt 24/24-watt bulb on 1958 models, or a Lucas No. 312 6-volt 30/24-watt bulb on 1959–64 models. Both these type bulbs have a broad locating flange and can be fitted in the bulb holder in one position only; a notch on the flange engages a projection on the bulb holder. The adaptor which secures the No. 166 or 312 Lucas main bulb can also be fitted in one position only, since its prongs are not symmetrical. Having fitted a new main bulb in its holder, engage the projections on the inside of the adaptor with the slots in the bulb holder, and secure the adaptor by turning it *clockwise*.

The parking bulb can be removed complete with its sprung holder by pulling it straight out of the reflector in which it is a push fit. If renewal is necessary, fit a Lucas No. 988 6-volt 3-watt single-contact bulb to the holder and push the latter into the hole near the bottom of the reflector.

If a headlamp glass requires renewing, it is necessary to fit a new light-unit comprising the glass *and* reflector. The headlamp rim can be detached from the old light-unit after prising the ends of the five wire clips out of the inner edge of the headlamp rim. After replacing the headlamp rim and the light-unit, firmly tighten the securing screw at the base of the rim.

The Lucas Headlamp (Arrow). The previous instructions given for the Leader headlamp apply also to the Arrow headlamp (type MCH 56) (which is not housed in a cowl and has no beam trimmer) except for the following details.

To remove the light-unit and rim, with the handlebars in their normal position, loosen the screw at the top of the rim and ease off the rim by pulling it forward at the top. The same type of Lucas bulbs as required for the Leader are suitable.

If the headlamp has to be set to obtain a beam centre parallel with the road, loosen the two lamp-securing bolts and tilt the headlamp as required. Afterwards firmly retighten the securing bolts.

Lighting Switch Positions. The lighting switch is mounted on the instrument panel or on top of the headlamp (*see* Figs. 9, 10) in the case of a Leader or Arrow respectively. The switch has the following three positions—

Headlamp, tail lamp, and speedometer light switched off.
Headlamp parking bulb, tail lamp, and speedometer light switched on.
Headlamp double-filament main bulb, tail lamp, and speedometer light switched on.

Note that battery charging while riding occurs in *all* the above three lighting-switch positions.

The Stop-tail Light. The Lucas stop-tail lamp (type 564) fitted to the Leader and Arrow embodies a reflex reflector. To obtain access to the bulb holder, remove the two screws which secure the rear portion of the lamp to the front portion. To remove the bulb from its holder, push the bulb inwards, turn slightly *anticlockwise*, and withdraw. When bulb renewal is necessary, the correct bulb to fit is a Lucas No. 352 6-volt, 18/13-watt double-filament, bayonet-fitting bulb.

When fitting a new bulb, note that the bulb base has offset pegs and therefore will enter the bulb holder in one position only. Push the bulb in and turn it *clockwise* in its holder. Afterwards replace the rear portion of the lamp and do not omit the rubber joint washer. The lens is in two sections. Fit the clear section at the bottom into the two slots provided in the red section. To secure the rear portion of the lamp, replace the two securing srews and tighten them firmly. Avoid excessive tightening.

Flasher Lamps (Leader). Where flasher indicators (an optional extra) are provided it may occasionally be necessary to renew one of the lamp

THE LUCAS LIGHTING SYSTEM 43

bulbs. Four lamps are attached to the machine. To renew a bulb withdraw the lens from the flasher lamp after removing the two securing screws, lightly press down on the bulb, and then turn the bulb in either

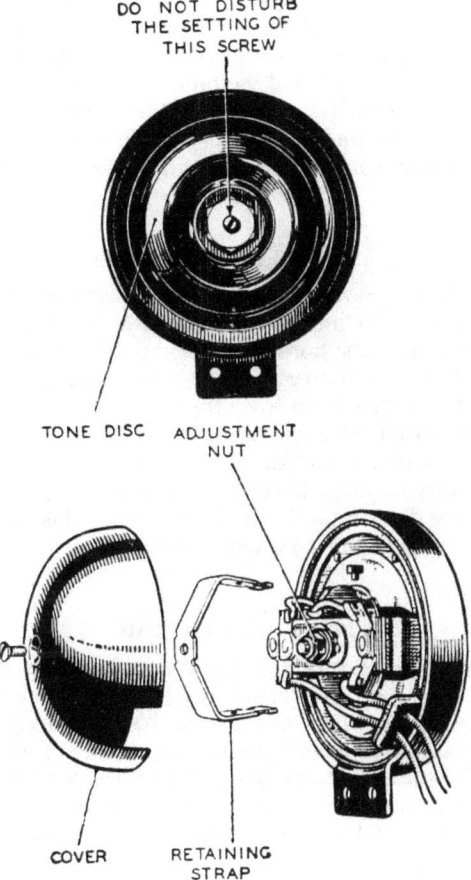

FIG. 23. THE LUCAS ELECTRIC HORN SHOWING ADJUSTMENT NUT
This horn (type HF1849) is fitted to the Leader and Arrow.

direction to free it. The correct type of bulb to fit is a Lucas No. 317 6-volt, 18-watt single-contact bulb with bayonet type fixing. Push a new bulb into its holder, with the pegs located each side of the holder, and then turn the bulb to lock its pegs in the holder. Afterwards replace the flasher lamp lens and tighten the two securing screws.

Warning Lights (Leader). On a Leader provided with front and rear flasher lamps to indicate turning direction, a warning light is fitted on the near side of the instrument panel. It shows *amber* when the flasher lamps are functioning. Where a *neutral* indicator is provided, a second warning light is fitted on the off side of the instrument panel and this shows *white* when *neutral* is engaged and the ignition is switched on. Should either warning light bulb require to be renewed, insert one hand below the end of the instrument panel and pull the bulb sideways to free it. Then screw out the faulty bulb and fit a new Lucas No. 990 6-volt, 3-watt, screw-in type bulb. Push it into the bulb holder and simultaneously screw it home. Then push the holder, with the new bulb fitted, into the body of the warning light.

THE ELECTRIC HORN

A Lucas type HF1849 horn is fitted to the Leader and Arrow and rarely needs any attention. At infrequent intervals a *slight* adjustment may be required to ensure that the horn continues to function at its best.

Referring to Fig. 23, to make an adjustment to the horn, first remove the horn cover and retaining strap from the rear of the horn. Then with the horn operating, with a 2BA spanner turn the adjustment nut slowly *anti-clockwise* until you obtain the best performance. Normally it is necessary to turn the nut very slightly. Do not interfere with the slotted screw in the centre of the tone disc on the front of the horn. This screw is accurately adjusted by the makers and a lock-nut secures it in position.

WIRING OF EQUIPMENT

Do not interfere with the wiring system unless you have very good reason for doing so. If you do disconnect any leads or make any alterations, first disconnect the *negative* lead at the battery. Inspect the braided wiring harness occasionally and see that no chafing of any of the leads is taking place. If necessary, tape up a chafed portion with insulating tape. The various cables can be identified by sleeve colours, and Lucas wiring diagrams for Leader and Arrow machines are included on pages 45, 46.

SLEEVE COLOURS, FIGS. 24 AND 25

B. Black	R. Red	W. White
U. Blue	P. Purple	Y. Yellow
N. Brown	G. Green	L. Light

When a cable has two colour code letters, the first indicates the main colour, and the second denotes the tracer colour.

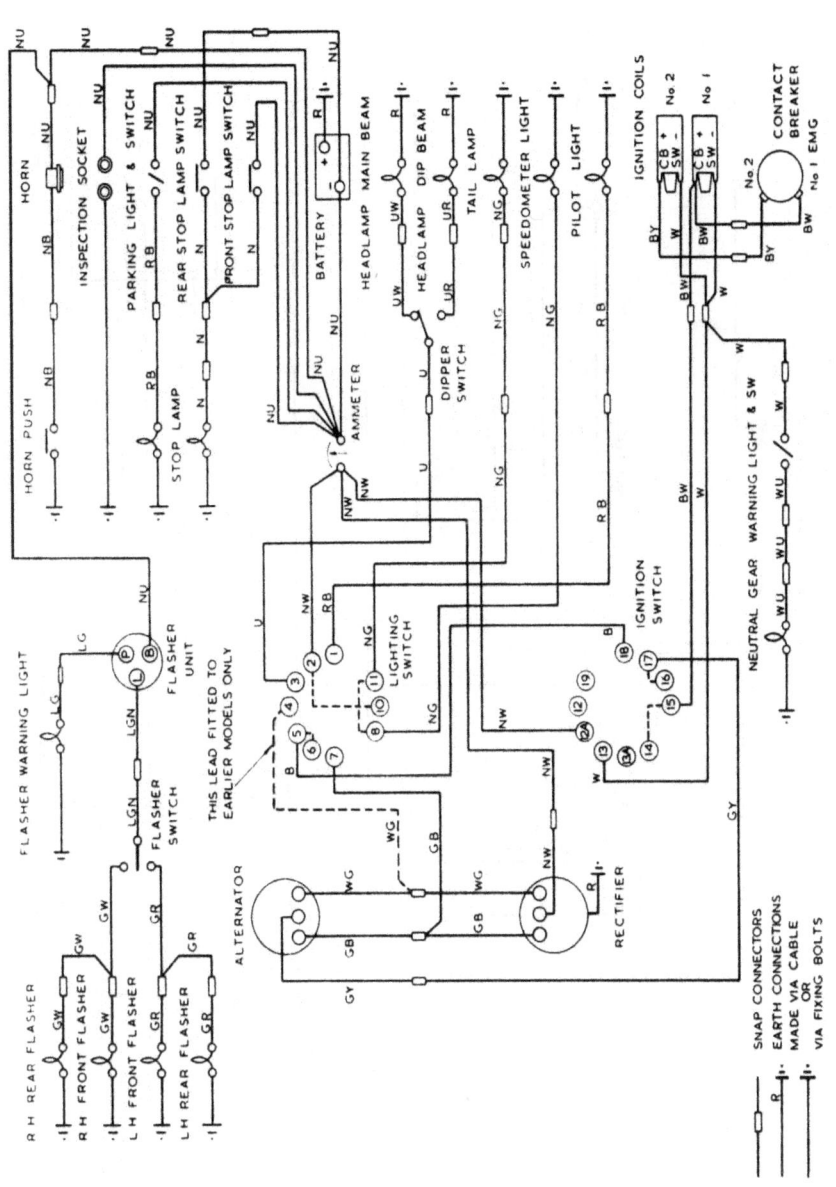

Fig. 24. Lucas Wiring Diagram for the Ariel Leader

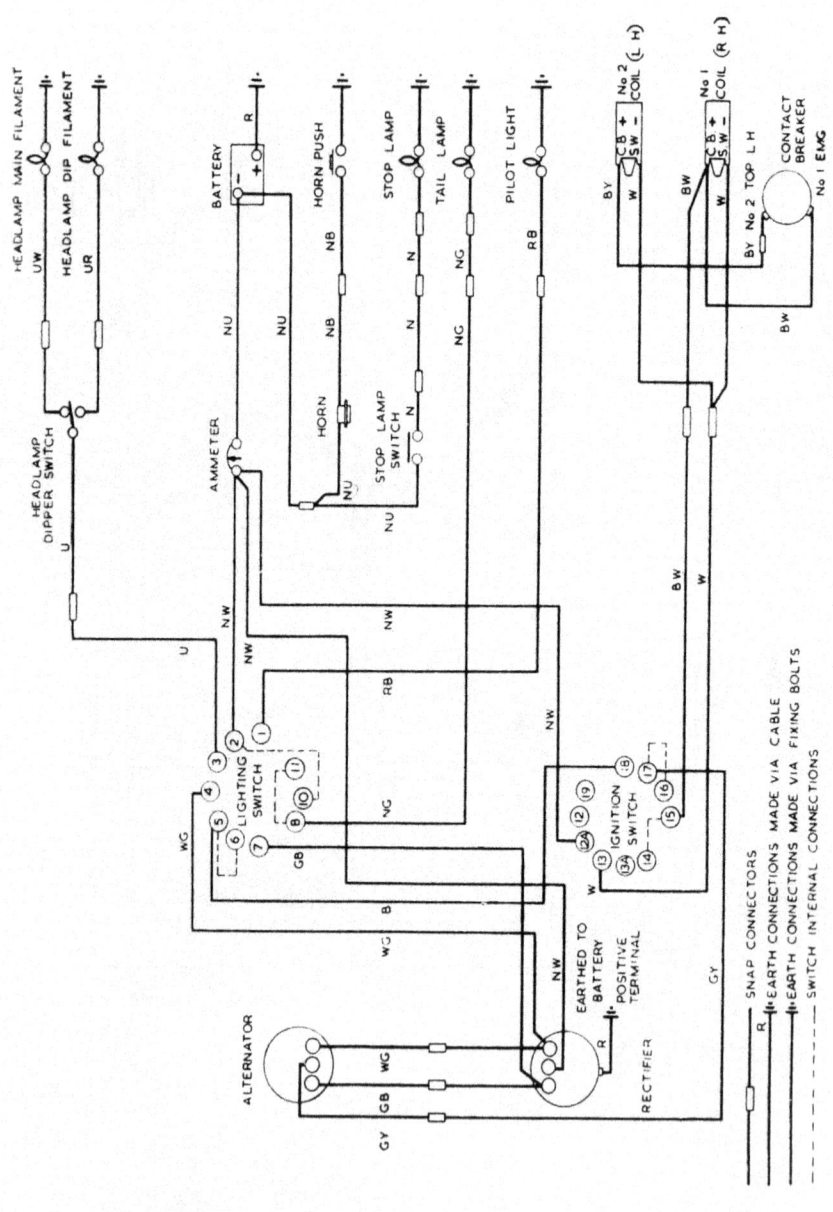

FIG. 25. LUCAS WIRING DIAGRAM FOR THE ARIEL ARROW

CHAPTER V

GENERAL MAINTENANCE

THIS chapter contains full maintenance instructions for all 1958–66 Ariel Leader and Arrow two-stroke models, except instructions already given in Chapters II, III, IV concerning lubrications, carburation and the lighting system respectively. Note that instructions without the prefix *Leader* or *Arrow* apply to both models.

Ariel Repairs and Spares. Should you have occasion to forward or deliver parts to the manufacturers (Ariel Motors Ltd., Armoury Road, Birmingham, 11; phone number: Birmingham, Victoria 5642) for repair always attach to *each* part a label on which is clearly written your full name and address. To obtain prompt attention, all correspondence concerning spares and technical advice should be written on separate sheets, each bearing your name and address.

Always quote the chassis or engine prefix letter and number, according to the nature of the part involved. Refer to the identification plate riveted to the chassis or frame beneath the dualseat.

There are numerous firms in the United Kingdom who can supply Ariel Leader and Arrow spares over the counter, and many appointed Ariel dealers who specialize in the overhaul and repair of Ariel two-stroke engines. Useful addresses may be found in the advertisement pages of *Motor Cycle*.

Some London Accessory Firms. Among reputable London firms (some of which have provincial branches) handling motor-cycle accessories, tools, clothing, etc. may be mentioned: Whitbys of Acton Ltd.; Claude Rye Ltd.; E. S. Motors; The Halford Cycle Co. Ltd.; Turner's Stores; James Grose Ltd.; Marble Arch Motor Supplies Ltd.; Pride & Clarke Ltd.; and George Grose Ltd. The purchase of good quality clothing is most important.

Clean and Polish Your Machine Regularly. This is important as it protects and maintains the finish in the best condition. It also reduces depreciation. Never dry clean the enamelled exterior parts. First wash them with warm water to remove dirt, etc. The use of detergents is not advised. A cloth moistened with turpentine can be used for removing any tar spots. Having thoroughly washed all enamelled parts, dry them with a chamois leather and afterwards polish with one of the well known makes of car polish.

Wash chromium-plated parts with warm water, dry with a chamois leather and then polish with a soft duster. On no account use metal polish. To remove any stains use a well known brand of chromium cleaner. To reduce tarnishing in winter it is a good plan to wipe over the chromium plated surfaces with a soft rag soaked in Tekall, obtainable in half-pint and one-pint tins at most garages. For cleaning the windscreen always use a genuine Perspex cleaner, and for cleaning the dualseat cover use nothing but warm soapy water.

Clean the hubs, spokes and the power unit with one of the popular oil and grease solvents. See that no solvent enters the electrical equipment or carburettor when applying and washing off the solvent.

To Retouch Enamelled Surfaces. Note that for retouching damaged or scratched enamel surfaces tins of synthetic enamel are available in all Leader and Arrow colours. The enamel takes about an hour to dry and should be applied with a small pointed brush indoors in a dust-free atmosphere. Before retouching any parts thoroughly clean them and afterwards wipe over with a cloth damped with cellulose thinner.

Removing L.H. Side Panel (Leader). Almost all engine and primary drive adjustments can be made by removing the near-side side panel. Five screws with rubber washers secure it. Four of them are clearly visible on the side of the machine, and it is only necessary to loosen them with a coin until they float freely. Circlips prevent their falling out. However, completely remove the fifth screw located at the rear end of the side panel just above the silencer. Then carefully remove the side panel, easing it over the cold-starting device knob, the fuel tap knob, and the pillion footrest.

Replacing L.H. Side Panel (Leader). Turn on the fuel tap and pull out the knob for the cold-starting device to the starting position. Now pass the side panel over the pillion footrest and behind the forward footrest and position the panel so that the knob for the cold-starting device and also the fuel tap project through the holes provided in the panel. Finally tighten the five panel-securing screws and reposition the knob and tap.

Removing R.H. Side Panel (Leader). The off-side side panel is secured by five screws similarly to the near-side panel. First withdraw the kickstarter and gear change levers, both of which are secured to serrated shafts by pinch bolts and nuts. Remove the bolts and nuts completely before easing the levers off. Ease the gear-change lever half way along its shaft and then rotate it to the vertical position. Footrest removal is then unnecessary. Now unscrew the five securing screws with a coin and ease the side panel over the pillion footrest, and withdraw from the machine.

Replacing R.H. Side Panel (Leader). Pass the off-side panel over the pillion footrest and behind the forward footrest. Next position it so that the gear-change lever and kick-starter lever shafts project through the holes provided in the panel and fit the five securing screws. Replace partially the gear-change lever by positioning it vertically on its shaft, turn to the position required, and press the lever properly on its shaft. Replace the kick-starter lever in the position required. See that it does not foul the gear-change lever at the end of its movement. Finally fit and securely tighten the pinch bolts which secure both levers.

FIG. 26. SHOWING QUICKLY DETACHABLE ENGINE COVER ON THE ARROW

The cover is secured by only one screw and one bolt and its removal gives access to the gearbox filler, level and drain plugs, and also the clutch adjuster. Note the rubber grommet behind the foot gear-change lever. Its removal gives access to the gearbox level plug for topping-up purposes.

Where Panniers Are Provided. Be careful when fitting or removing a side panel not to damage the enamel finish on the panel.

To Remove Engine Cover (Arrow). On the Arrow, which has no side panels, removal of the engine cover gives access to the gearbox oil filler, the level and drain plugs, and the clutch adjuster.

To remove the engine cover first withdraw the gear-change and kick-starter levers which are fitted to serrated shafts and secured with pinch bolts. The latter must be completely removed. When removing the gear-change lever rotate it to the vertical position as previously described in the paragraph dealing with the removal of the off-side panel on the Leader. Footrest removal is then unnecessary. Now remove the bolt which passes through the front end of the cover and into the crankcase. Then remove the screw from the centre of the engine cover and carefully ease the cover off.

To Replace Engine Cover (Arrow). Check that there is one felt washer fitted to the kick-starter shaft and two on the gear-change shaft. Then position the engine cover. See that no cables are trapped or pinched. Now fit the bolt with a plain washer under its head through the bracket on the engine cover and into the front of the crankcase. Finally fit the screw with a plain washer under its head through the centre of the engine cover and into the adaptor on the gearbox.

THE IGNITION SYSTEM

This section deals with electrical components concerned solely with ignition, namely the sparking plugs, the coils, and the contact-breaker. The components concerned with ignition *and* lighting, namely the type RM 13/15 alternator, the rectifier, and the ML9E battery are dealt with in Chapter IV.

Suitable Sparking Plugs. To obtain maximum engine performance throughout the throttle range, plus easy starting, it is essential always to run on a suitable type of sparking plug. Those recommended by Ariel Motors Ltd. are—

Lodge—Fit a two-point non-detachable type 2HLN.
Champion—Fit a two-point non-detachable type N3.

The above mentioned types of sparking plugs have been recommended after extensive bench and road tests and should be serviceable for a very considerable time. Regular inspection should be made so see whether their gaps are correct and the plugs clean. On removing the plugs the earthing point should be a dark grey colour, with the mouth of the plug only slightly sooted. If a plug is thickly coated with carbon, or wet, this suggests an oily mixture in the combustion chamber. In this case check that the correct petroil mixture is being used (*see* page 10). The petrol-oil ratio must be correct. It is a good plan to carry a spare plug in case of trouble suddenly developing while riding. Black plastic covers attach the high tension leads to the plugs and this prevents any water getting on the plug terminals while riding.

The Sparking Plug Gap. It is important to maintain the correct gap between the sparking plug electrodes and it is advisable to check the gap

GENERAL MAINTENANCE

for each sparking plug about every 3,000 miles. The gap between the centre electrode and the outer earthed point should be not less than 0·030 in. and not more than 0·040 in. When re-gapping a plug it is desirable for obvious reasons to set its gap at or near the bottom limit.

Check the gap with a suitable feeler gauge. Gauges are obtainable in sets from most motor-cycle agents or tool dealers. A 0·030-in. gauge should be a nice sliding fit. When adjusting the gap, never attempt to bend or tap the centre electrode. Use a plug re-gapping tool (*see* Fig. 27) which is made by the plug manufacturers. Fit the tool on the earthing point and lever it closer to, or away from, the centre electrode as required to adjust the gap to the correct width.

Cleaning the Sparking Plugs. When running-in a new or rebored engine it is advisable to remove and check the plugs for cleanliness about every

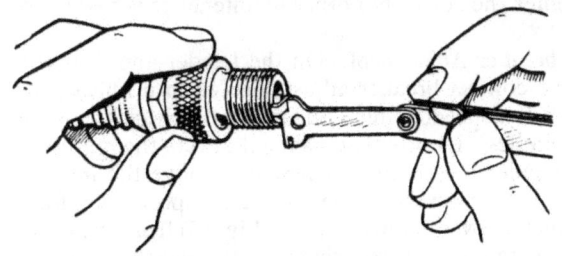

FIG. 27. USING A TYPICAL SPARKING PLUG RE-GAPPING TOOL

500 miles, but normally it is quite sufficient to clean the plugs about every 3,000 miles, assuming that carburation is correct and the engine is running on the correct petrol-oil ratio.

Quick cleaning of a plug can be done by brushing the points with a small wire brush and lightly rubbing their firing sides with some smooth emery cloth. The best method of thoroughly cleaning a plug is to hand it to a garage and have it cleaned and tested with special equipment such as an air-blast unit. In a few minutes the plug can be thoroughly cleaned of all deposits, washed, and tested for sparking at a pressure exceeding 100 lb. per sq in. The Lodge and Champion sparking plugs recommended for Leader and Arrow motor-cycles are of the non-detachable type and it is not possible to dismantle the plugs for cleaning.

Replacing a Plug. Before doing this renew the copper washer if it is worn or flattened, and clean the plug threads. It is a good plan to coat the threads with some graphite paste before replacing a plug. Screw the plug home by hand as far as possible, and always use the plug spanner in the tool kit for final tightening. Avoid using excessive force. Never fit a sparking plug that is in any way damaged.

Simple Method of Testing Plugs. If the engine refuses to start or runs erratically it is easy to test the plugs. Remove both of them and, with the high-tension leads fitted, place the plugs so that their threaded portions are in contact with the fins of the cylinder head, and with the firing points visible. Switch on the ignition, depress the kick-starter quickly several times and note if sparks occur regularly between the plug firing points. With the plugs removed it is very easy to turn over the engine quickly. The sparks should be clearly visible. They can also be heard.

The Ignition Coils. One coil is provided for each cylinder. The coils are secured inside the frame and are accessible through the hole in the bottom of the glove compartment on the Leader and Arrow. Occasionally check that the high tension leads are in good condition and securely fitted into the coils. Also check that the rubber covers are in place where the leads enter the coils. No other maintenance is necessary.

Contact-breaker Adjustment. On the Leader and Arrow it is advisable to check the contact-breaker adjustment when a mileage of 500 miles is recorded on the speedometer. Subsequently check the adjustment about every 5,000 miles. Incorrect adjustment affects the ignition timing.

On the Leader it is necessary first to remove the near-side side panel (*see* page 48). Then on the Leader and Arrow proceed as follows. Remove the round metal cover (shown at (6) in Fig. 15) from the primary chaincase after unscrewing the three securing screws. Slip the cover a few inches up the lead which passes through it. On certain engines you can remove the cover completely. The two pairs of contacts are now accessible. The *inner* contacts are those which are adjustable.

Turn the engine over slowly by gently operating the kick-starter until the contact-breaker cam fully opens the upper pair of contacts. When the contacts are wide open the gap between the contacts should be 0·014 in.–0·016 in. Measure the gap with a suitable feeler gauge and adjust the gap if it varies from that just stated. If an adjustment is necessary, slacken the slotted sleeve nut located on the mounting plate within the looped spring. Then move the inner contact as required to increase or reduce the gap. After making an adjustment tighten the sleeve nut and while doing so be sure that the inner contact does not move. Finally again check the gap between the two contacts to make sure that it is correct. Having checked and if necessary adjusted the gap between the top pair of contacts, check and if necessary adjust the gap between the bottom contacts in a similar manner.

Cleaning the Contacts. When checking the gap between the contacts always inspect the contacts closely and, if they need cleaning, do this *before* finally adjusting the gap. If the contacts have a grey, frosted appearance, it can be reasonably assumed that they are in good condition.

GENERAL MAINTENANCE

Should the contacts be only slightly discoloured, clean them with a cloth moistened with petrol. If the contacts are blackened or pitted, clean them thoroughly with a fine carborundum stone, or if one is not available, with *very fine* emery cloth. Afterwards completely remove all traces of metallic dust with a petrol-moistened cloth. When cleaning and dressing contacts (seldom necessary), it is essential to remove the minimum amount of contact metal necessary to ensure: (a) brightness of the contacts, (b) parallelism of the contacts, (c) perfect smoothness and truth of the contact faces.

Replacing Contact-breaker Cover. Be careful to position the lead coloured *black and white*, and connected to the bottom pair of contacts, *rearward* and around the lower loop spring. This will prevent the lead becoming chafed by the moving parts of the contact-breaker unit. Do not forget to fit the joint washer between the contact-breaker cover and the primary chaincase and see that the leads which pass through the cover are to the rear of the cover top securing-screw. On the Leader it remains to replace the nearside panel as described on page 48.

To Remove Contact-breaker Assembly. This is rarely necessary. To remove the assembly after removing the contact-breaker cover, pull apart the two snap connectors in the leads from the contact-breaker and remove the two screws and plain washers which secure the contact-breaker mounting plate to the primary chaincase. The contact-breaker assembly can then be withdrawn. Note that when replacing the contact-breaker assembly the condenser with the lead coloured *black and yellow* must be uppermost. The cam which operates the contact breaker is secured by a single captive screw. A circlip retains it in the cam.

The Ignition Timing. The standard ignition timing for both cylinders is such that the contacts just break with the piston 20 degrees before T.D.C. Do not experiment or interfere with the standard timing, as no other timing is satisfactory. Any slight variation in timing can be corrected by adjusting the contact-breaker gap. Thus it is permissible to have a gap of 0·014 in. for one set of contacts and 0·016 in. for the other set. To check the ignition timing proceed as below.

Remove both the sparking plugs and the contact-breaker cover, and check the gap between the contacts with the latter fully open. If necessary, adjust the gap for both pairs of contacts to 0·015 in. To determine the exact moment of opening of a set of contacts it is a good plan to use a 6-volt lamp. Connect one lead from the lamp to a good earth point on the engine or frame, and connect the other lead to the appropriate rocker arm return spring. The circuit is then complete and with the ignition switched on the lamp should light when the contacts open. The ammeter can also be used as an alternative. It will indicate a discharge when the contacts are closed with the ignition switched on. Immediately the contacts open, with the ignition switched on, the ammeter needle returns to zero.

Place the machine in 4th gear and turn the engine by rotating the rear wheel until the lamp lights or the ammeter records zero. At this point insert the ignition timing peg (Part No. 3557), included in the tool kit, through the hole for the top screw securing the contact-breaker cover. It should engage and enter a hole drilled in the flywheel. Adjust the contact-breaker gap if necessary, or rotate the contact-breaker plate so that the lamp just goes out or the ammeter reads zero when the ignition timing peg engages the drilled hole in the flywheel. Repeat the above procedure on the second cylinder and adjust if necessary its relative contact-breaker gap.

DECARBONIZING

The exact time at which the removal of carbon deposits becomes necessary depends to some extent on riding conditions. Excessive carbon deposits cause a tendency for knocking when accelerating quickly or hill climbing, and a general deterioration in performance occurs. To continue riding when decarbonizing is required is extremely bad for the engine. Under normal circumstances it is advisable to decarbonize every 5,000 miles. Carbon deposits form on top of the pistons and inside the cylinder heads, exhaust ports, and silencers. It is necessary for decarbonizing to dismantle the exhaust system, and the cylinder heads, and advisable to remove the cylinder barrels, and the pistons. Before beginning to dismantle the engine obtain the following spares: two cylinder-head gaskets, two cylinder-base washers, two exhaust-sealing rings, and two silencer-end seals.

Removing the Exhaust System. Where a Leader is concerned remove both side panels and the legshields. Remove the two nuts and screws securing the rear stop lamp switch to the offside silencer bracket; leave the loose switch dangling by its leads and spring. Now on a Leader loosen the acorn nuts at the extremities of the silencers just enough to free the silencers from the support stay. Then loosen the nuts on the silencer clamp bolts where they join the exhaust pipe, and pull both silencers to the rear. On an Arrow remove completely the silencer acorn nuts, loosen the silencer clamp bolts, and slide the silencers forward to free them from the support stays. Then withdraw the silencers to the rear.

With the "C" spanner provided in the tool kit unscrew the gland nut for the exhaust pipe from each cylinder-barrel exhaust port. Note the sealing gland inside each exhaust port. This should be renewed if damaged. Free each footrest and exhaust-pipe bracket after removing the inner nut which secures them to the crankcase. Then withdraw both exhaust pipes.

Removing the Cylinder Heads. Remove the plastic covers and high-tension leads from both sparking plugs. Afterwards remove both plugs

GENERAL MAINTENANCE

with a box spanner and tommy-bar and place them aside with their washers for inspection and cleaning. With the hexagon socket key provided in the tool kit remove the four sleeve nuts which secure each cylinder head. Loosen the four nuts first in a diagonal order. When using the socket key fit the short arm of the key into the socket heads of the cylinder head bolts. Carefully lift off each cylinder head from the cylinder barrel after removing the four sleeve nuts. Examine the special aluminium gasket fitted between each head and barrel. If not in perfect condition a new gasket must be fitted on assembly.

Removing the Cylinder Barrels. After removing the cylinder heads it is a simple matter to withdraw the two barrels. When pulling each barrel away from the crankcase face, be careful not to turn it, and support the piston as it emerges from the barrel mouth. It may otherwise become damaged through falling sharply backwards or forwards.

Removing the Pistons. On no account must the pistons be interchanged. It is therefore advisable to remove them one at a time to prevent accidental replacement in the wrong cylinder. If both pistons are removed one after the other attach a label for identification. Each piston is secured to the connecting-rod by a fully floating gudgeon-pin and removal is simple.

Cover the mouth of the crankcase below the pistons with a large clean cloth to prevent the possibility of anything falling into the crankcase. The ends of each gudgeon-pin are positioned by spring wire circlips in the piston bosses. Remove both circlips. To remove a circlip use a pair of pointed-nosed pliers to grip the turned up ends of the circlip and squeeze them together. Now push out the gudgeon-pin, preferably using a piece of half-inch diameter wooden dowel about six inches long. While pushing out the gudgeon-pin support the piston on the opposite side. Do not use force and if the pin is a tight fit on a fairly new engine, heat the piston by wrapping it in a cloth dipped in boiling water. After removing the gudgeon-pin the piston can be lifted off the small-end of the connecting-rod.

Removing Carbon Deposits. Carefully remove all carbon deposits from the top and inside of each piston. To prevent the light alloy surface becoming scratched or damaged it is best to remove the carbon with a stick of soft solder having a sharp edge. Afterwards polish the piston crown with a pad of wire wool. Good quality metal polish can be used, but all polish must afterwards be carefully removed. Do not scrape the sides of the piston or the lands between the piston-ring grooves. Never use emery cloth for polishing the pistons. Polishing of the skirt can be done with metal polish, but clean thoroughly afterwards.

With a stick of soft solder, as used for the piston, thoroughly scrape off all carbon deposits from the insides of both cylinder heads which like the pistons are made of aluminium alloy. Make sure that the threads in the holes for the sparking plugs are absolutely clean and free from carbon particles. Polish the combustion chamber surfaces with a pad of wire

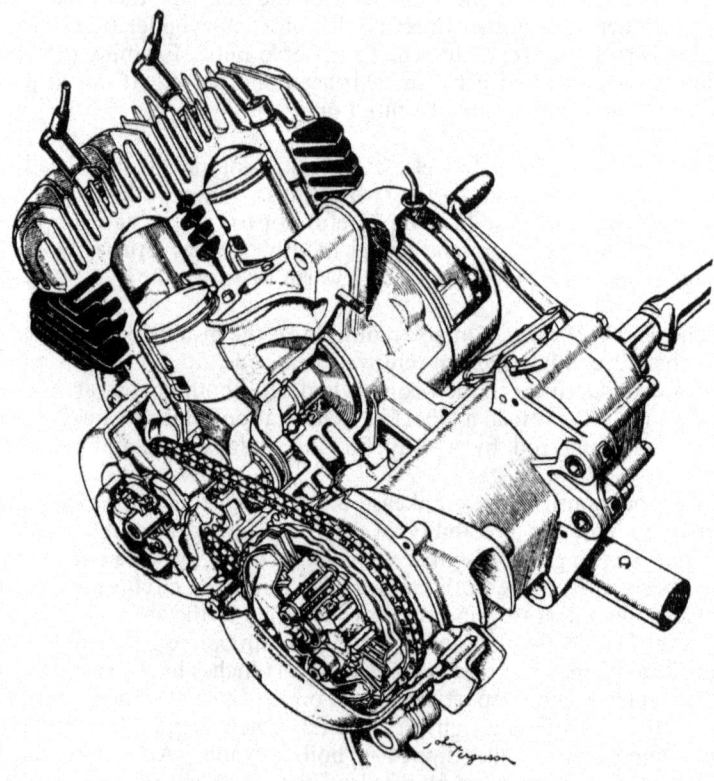

FIG. 28. SHOWING DETAILS OF THE 249 C.C. ARIEL TRANSVERSE TWIN TWO-STROKE POWER UNIT
(*By courtesy of "Motor Cycle," London*)

wool or metal polish. Remove all carbon from the exhaust ports of the cylinder barrels. The barrels are not of light alloy and it is permissible to scrape the ports with a proprietary scraper. Fine emery cloth wrapped around one finger can be used to remove the carbon from inside the curved exhaust ports, but be careful not to touch the inner wall of a cylinder barrel. As far as possible remove carbon deposits from the ends of both exhaust pipes.

GENERAL MAINTENANCE 57

Dealing with Each Silencer. Remove the acorn nut from the end of the silencer. Next remove the thin lock-nut positioned immediately in front of the acorn nut. Then withdraw the small cone-shaped alloy die casting and the alloy end-section from the silencer. With a screwdriver prise out the sealing ring located between the alloy end-section and the main silencer body. Where an earlier round type of baffle assembly is provided, remove the assembly for cleaning. When convenient it is desirable to change to the latest type baffle assembly. With this type it is not necessary to remove the baffle assembly unless damaged or until a big mileage has been covered. With a suitably pointed screwdriver or bar you can clean out the holes in the end baffle which can be observed between the inner tube and the silencer body.

Assemble the silencer correctly. The centre stud must pass through the small diameter tube of the baffle assembly. Fit the stud from the exhaust-pipe end and see that the stud passes through the locating plate in the silencer body. Renew the sealing ring and fit the ring into the end of the silencer body, followed by the silencer end-section and its centre tube. Now fit the cone-shaped alloy die casting over the stud protruding from the silencer end-section; also fit and carefully tighten the thin lock-nut on the silencer centre stud. Fit the acorn nut, but tighten only slightly.

If the Cylinder Barrels are not Removed. In order to remove all carbon deposits safely and thoroughly the removal of the cylinder barrels and pistons is desirable. But this is not absolutely essential. It is permissible if care is taken to remove the cylinder heads every 5,000 miles and the barrels and pistons every 10,000 miles. If the cylinder barrels are not removed, smear a light coating of grease around the top of each cylinder bore and turn the engine until one piston is at T.D.C. Cover the other cylinder bore to keep out any particles of carbon and carefully remove all carbon deposits, as previously described, from the top of the piston. Afterwards polish the crown. Repeat the procedure for the other piston. After cleaning both pistons wipe away all traces of grease which will have prevented carbon particles penetrating between the cylinder bores and the tops of the pistons.

When removing carbon from an exhaust port make sure that the piston completely uncovers the port. Blow away any carbon dust which remains and wipe out the cylinder bore with a clean rag *before* turning the engine to tackle the other exhaust port.

The Piston Rings. When occasion is had to remove the pistons it is desirable also to remove the piston rings and clean the grooves in which they fit. Polish the grooves with metal polish. The two compression rings should also be closely examined as their good condition is extremely important. The rings should show good bore contact which is indicated by a matt grey finish. Renewal is called for when there is any discoloration of the bearing surface. The same applies when the rings become vertically slack in their grooves. The gap between the ends of a ring when the latter is on the piston and in the cylinder bore is also important. Renew a ring where the gap excees 0·004 in. It is generally advisable to fit new rings every alternate decarbonizing. On a new engine the gap is 0·008 in. − 0·010 in. + the diameter of the locating peg 0·0625 in. Clean thoroughly the inside faces and the ends of both rings.

The piston rings being made of cast-iron, are exceedingly vulnerable and great care must be taken when removing them from the pistons. It is desirable not to interchange the rings. When removing a ring it should not be sprung out appreciably wider than the piston diameter, otherwise it will break. Remove the *top* compression ring first. With the thumbs spring the ends of the ring slightly apart so that the ring is expanded enough to lift it up clear of the piston. Remove the second piston ring in a similar manner. When removing the rings or cleaning a piston on no account scratch or in any way damage the piston. Never clamp it in a vice. Replace the piston rings in the same grooves from which they were removed and be careful not to spring the ends of the rings out too widely. See that the pegs in the ring grooves are located between the ends of the rings.

Fitting the Pistons. Each piston must be fitted to the connecting rod from which it was removed and must be fitted the right way round. The front side is indicated by an arrow and the word FRONT stamped on the piston crown. Incidentally, when a piston is correctly fitted the port on each side of it is lightly offset forward of the gudgeon-pin. Offer up the correct piston the right way round to the appropriate connecting-rod small-end and insert the correct gudgeon-pin after oiling it. Fit new circlips unless the old ones are perfect to secure the gudgeon-pin. See that the groove for one circlip is visible on the piston and with a pair of pointed-nosed pliers ease the circlip home into its groove, using a rotary movement to ensure that it beds down snugly. This is very important. Fit a circlip on the other side of the gudgeon-pin in a similar manner. Then replace the second piston, making sure that it is fitted the right way round.

Replacing the Cylinder Barrels. First make sure that both cylinder base washers are in sound condition. Renew them if not. Paper washers are used. Smear the skirt of the piston to which the cylinder barrel is to be fitted with some clean engine oil. Then hold the correct cylinder barrel over the piston with the barrel the correct way round and gently slide it over the piston, lowering it carefully and slowly. To enable the piston rings to enter the bore, squeeze the rings with a thumb and one finger inserted through the small cut at the front and rear of the bottom of the cylinder barrel skirt. If the piston rings do not enter easily do not press down on the cylinder barrel, but squeeze the rings together until they

GENERAL MAINTENANCE 59

glide into the cylinder bore, and the cylinder barrel can be slid home over the whole piston on to the crankcase. Then fit the second cylinder barrel in a similar manner.

Fitting the Cylinder Heads. Unless the old cylinder head gaskets are in perfect condition, fit new ones. Then position the two heads on top of the gaskets. Fit a plain washer under the head of each of the eight socket-head cylinder-head sleeve nuts. Next fit the sleeve nuts through the holes in the top of the cylinder heads and on to the studs protruding from the top of the crankcase. With the hexagon socket key screw down loosely all the sleeve nuts. Then with each cylinder head tighten down the four sleeve nuts evenly in a diagonal order. This will avoid any risk of distorting the cylinder head.

Replace both sparking plugs. It is assumed that they have been cleaned and that their electrode gaps are correct. A little graphite grease smeared on the threads of the plugs will assist future removal. Connect up the high-tension leads to both plugs.

Replacing the Exhaust System. Replace the two exhaust pipes first. Fit the exhaust pipe securing nuts on to the pipes and then fit new sealing washers at the cylinder barrel exhaust ports. A soft iron washer should be fitted, not the earlier copper and asbestos type washer. Position the exhaust pipes into the exhaust ports of the cylinder barrels and fit the exhaust pipe brackets over the inner footrest securing studs. Then with the "C" spanner screw the exhaust pipe securing nuts into the cylinder barrel exhaust ports. Tighten the two nuts firmly after making sure that the exhaust pipes are as close together as possible below the engine.

Fit a plain washer, a shake-proof washer, and a nut to the two inner footrest studs and firmly tighten both nuts. Now slide the silencers over the rear ends of the exhaust pipes and locate them into the support stay at the rear of the machine. Finally tighten both silencer clamp bolts and the acorn nuts at the ends of the silencers. Where a Leader is concerned, replace the leg shields and the two side panels.

MAJOR ENGINE OVERHAUL

Major engine overhaul involving such things as dismantling of the crankshaft assembly, renewal of engine bearings, etc. should be entrusted to an appointed Ariel dealer fully equipped to handle this work. Special tools and experience are required. Note the following points.

The Alternator. This has no wearing parts and its removal is only necessary when the crankshaft requires attention. If for any reason you remove the rotor do not separate it from the stator for more than a few minutes, otherwise it may become demagnetized.

Worn Cylinders. Provided that the engine is run carefully and is properly lubricated, cylinder wear should take place *very* gradually, and excessive wear should not occur until a big mileage has been covered. The bores are of hard-wearing cast-iron. When excessive wear occurs it is necessary to have the cylinder barrels rebored and oversize pistons fitted. Two sizes are available and advantage can be taken of an exchange service scheme whereby a worn cylinder barrel can be part-exchanged for a rebored cylinder barrel, together with a suitable oversize piston complete with gudgeon-pin, rings, and circlips, ready for fitting to the engine.

The wear in the bore of a cylinder barrel becomes most pronounced at the front and rear of the upper half and it is desirable to have the cylinders rebored when the amount of wear exceeds 0·0035 in. The original bore size is 2·125 in. A bore gauge is necessary to check for cylinder wear.

Small-end Bushes. Generally these bushes last the life of the connecting-rods in which they are fitted. Thus it is unlikely that the bushes will need attention between general overhauls. When a crankshaft is reconditioned, new connecting-rods, complete with small-end bushes are included.

The Gearbox. This is in unit construction with the engine. If any trouble should be encountered it should be entrusted to an appointed Ariel dealer equipped with the necessary tools.

THE TRANSMISSION

The Ariel Clutch. A three-plate clutch of the "wet" type is fitted to the nearside end of the gearbox and completely enclosed by the primary chaincase. It is silent and smooth in operation and unless the clutch is badly used will give *long service* without trouble. It is practically indestructible. A transmission shock absorber is embodied in the clutch hub and normally this needs *no attention*. Should the shock absorber be dismantled for examination, it is essential when assembling it to replace the rubbers so that the thicker ones on each vane take the driving shock and are fitted to the *left-hand side* of the vane driving member when viewed from the back of the clutch hub.

The friction material used for the clutch is bonded to the friction plates and service-exchange plates are available for renewal purposes. Note that the clutch springs are retained by sleeve nuts which must always be fully tightened. The nuts are not designed for alteration of spring tension. The clutch adjustment on the offside of the gearbox must always be kept correct.

If Clutch Slip Occurs. Clutch slip must always be avoided as it causes damage and overheating. It is generally due to insufficient free movement in the clutch operating-mechanism. A method of testing for clutch slip is to place the machine on its stand, start up the engine, engage top gear, and then apply the rear brake. It should be possible to pull up the engine, even on full throttle, without the occurrence of clutch slip. After a very

GENERAL MAINTENANCE

big mileage the friction linings begin to wear thin and may cause the clutch to slip.

If clutch slip occurs check the clutch adjustment and if slip persists with the adjustment correct, dismantle the clutch plates after removing the primary chaincase. Linings which have a hard and glazed appearance require renewing. Clutch plates with new linings should be soaked in oil of the type used for the primary chaincase for about half an hour before replacement.

A dry clutch-operating rod is a possible cause of clutch slip when the

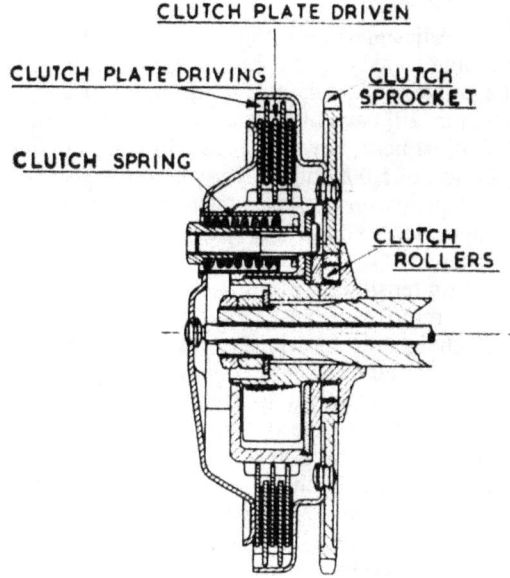

FIG. 29. SECTIONED VIEW OF ARIEL CLUTCH ASSEMBLY
(Ariel Motors Ltd.)

plates are in sound condition and clutch adjustment is correct. The remedy is to remove the rod and smear it with oil. Clutch drag, or failure of the clutch to disengage properly when operating the handlebar lever can be due to excessive free play in the clutch-operating mechanism or a broken operating rod.

Clutch Adjustment. Always maintain the correct clearance in the clutch-operating mechanism. There should be a minimum free movement of $\frac{1}{8}$ in. at the handlebar clutch control lever and $\frac{1}{16}$ in. clearance or end play between the clutch-operating lever and the push-rod passing through the gearbox mainshaft. During running-in an adjustment may be called for fairly early but after running-in adjustment is not frequently necessary.

To make a clutch adjustment first remove the off-side side panel on a Leader or the engine cover on an Arrow. Then remove the detachable plate, secured by two screws, which covers the gearbox filler hole and the push-rod adjuster. Slacken the lock-nut and turn the adjuster screw as required to provide the correct clutch adjustment between the clutch-operating lever and the push-rod. Afterwards securely tighten the lock-nut. To obtain sufficient free movement at the handlebar clutch-control lever, make the necessary adjustment by means of the screwed adjuster sleeve fitted to the clutch cable at the gearbox end of the cable. Finally replace the side panel or engine cover.

Primary Chain Adjustment. If the tension of the primary chain is permitted to become too slack, this results in the chain sprockets rapidly wearing. If the primary chaincase is regularly topped-up to the correct level, primary chain adjustment should only be necessary about every 5,000 miles. An adjustment, however, is usually necessary after completing the running-in period of 1,000 miles. The life of the primary chain as well as the sprockets depends on correct adjustment of tension and on lubrication. It is a good plan to check the chain tension each time you top-up the oilbath chaincase.

To check the chain tension first remove the nearside panel on a Leader. Then unscrew and remove the inspection cap (shown at (2) in Fig. 15) from the primary chaincase. Slowly turn the engine over by means of the kick-starter and check the tension at a number of places. Chain wear is often uneven. With the chain in its tightest position the total up and down movement should not exceed $\frac{5}{8}$ in. and be not less than $\frac{3}{8}$ in. Insufficient tension overloads the gearbox bearings and damages the chain. Adjust the chain tension as required.

The chain tension adjuster is located as shown at 8 in Fig. 15 at the forward edge of the primary chaincase. The adjuster comprises three components; a screw, a slotted plug, and a nylon adjuster sleeve. Remove the external screw and the slotted plug which is screwed into the chaincase. Then to tighten the chain turn the exposed nylon adjuster sleeve *clockwise*, and *anticlockwise* to slacken it. Use a screwdriver applied to the slot in the sleeve. When the correct chain tension is obtained replace the slotted plug and securely tighten it. Afterwards fit and firmly tighten the external screw and replace the chaincase inspection cap.

Note that if the external screw cannot be removed after unscrewing it four complete turns, tighten the slotted plug screwed into the chaincase to prevent the nylon adjuster sleeve from rotating. This precaution prevents the chain adjuster inside the chaincase being screwed apart, rendering it necessary to remove the primary chaincase in order to assemble the chain adjuster.

Secondary Chain Adjustment. Being completely enclosed in the rear chaincase and automatically lubricated, the secondary chain wears very

GENERAL MAINTENANCE

slowly. Its tension, however, should be checked regularly and an adjustment made where necessary. It is desirable to check the tension about every 1,000 miles. An actual adjustment is seldom necessary more often than every 3,000–4,000 miles. In connexion with chain tension, remember that a slack chain can cause damage to the chain and sprockets and is liable to jump off. An excessively taut chain causes rapid wear of the chain and sprockets.

Referring to Fig. 30, jack the machine up on its centre stand and remove

FIG. 30. SHOWING SECONDARY CHAIN ADJUSTMENT
1. Rubber grummet fitted to hole giving access to chain.
2. Rubber grummet fitted to hole giving access to three wheel securing nuts.
3. Wheel spindle nut.
4. Chain adjuster.
5. Lock-nut for (4).
6. Rear fork end.

the large rubber grummet shown at (1) from the chaincase. This gives access to the chain. Then rotate the rear wheel and check the chain tension with the chain in its tightest position. Move the chain up and down with one forefinger. The total up and down movement should be $1\frac{1}{4}$ in.–$1\frac{1}{2}$ in. To adjust the chain tension loosen the spindle nut (3) a few turns. Also slacken the special nut which secures the brake torque arm to the rear brake anchor plate. Now slacken the lock-nut (5) which secures the adjuster (4) in each rear fork (6). Then to tighten the chain screw out each adjuster until the chain tension is correct. To prevent the wheels becoming out of true alignment it is essential to screw out each adjuster the same number of turns. Then tighten the two adjuster lock-nuts, being careful not to turn the adjusters while doing this. Afterwards tighten the wheel spindle nut securely. While tightening the nut keep the tommy-bar on the offside end of the spindle vertical. Finally firmly tighten the special nut securing the brake torque arm to the brake anchor plate.

Repositioning the rear wheel may have altered the rear brake adjustment. Check and adjust if necessary (*see* page 66). Also check the alignment of the front and rear wheels.

Checking Wheel Alignment. The checking of wheel alignment after adjusting the secondary chain is always desirable because if the wheels have become out of alignment through unequal adjustment of the chain adjusters, the steering of the machine is affected. To check wheel alignment place the machine on its centre stand and, if available, use a straight-edge consisting of a six foot length of 3 in. × 1 in. planed wood. Place the straight-edge alongside the machine about seven inches from ground level, with the front wheel pointing straight ahead. It should contact each wheel at *two* points.

If no straight-edge is available, use a suitable length of string. Form a loop at one end and pass this over the stem of the tyre valve and round the rear tyre which should be positioned so that when the length of string is pulled forward to the front wheel it clears all obstructions. With the front wheel pointing straight ahead, and the string pulled tight, it should contact each wheel at two points. Make a check on each side of the machine.

Should an alignment check with a straight-edge or a piece of string prove that the wheels are not truly aligned, reposition the secondary chain adjusters until perfect alignment is obtained. It may be necessary to move only one chain adjuster. After moving the rear wheel the necessary amount, check the tension of the secondary chain as previously described.

Removal of Chaincase (Secondary Chain). To remove the chaincase for chain or rear wheel sprocket inspection or removal it is only necessary to remove four bolts and nuts which secure the quickly detachable chaincase. No gasket is fitted between the two halves.

Removal of Chaincase (Primary Chain). On a Leader first remove both side panels and on an Arrow remove the engine cover. Next remove the nearside footrest and the rear brake pedal. It is necessary prior to withdrawing the brake pedal from its housing to detach the brake pedal lever, just behind the gearbox, from the splined shaft. Remove the drain plug and allow all oil to drain off from the chaincase. Remove the contact-breaker cover and disconnect the two low tension cables at the snap connectors. To ensure correct assembly, note the "tracer" colours on the cables. The contact-breaker plate should not be disturbed or it will be necessary to retime the ignition. To avoid damaging the oil seal, remove the contact-breaker cam which is positioned by a locating peg. As the fixing screw is loosened the cam is extracted from its taper. Remove the primary chain adjuster by removing the external plug screw and the stop plug fitted into the front end of the chaincase. Screw the plug screw into the internal nylon adjusting sleeve and withdraw the adjusting sleeve. This releases the chain tensioner blade. Note the "O" ring oil seal on the nylon adjusting sleeve and prior to assembly see that it is correctly positioned. Finally remove the eight screws from around the edge of the primary

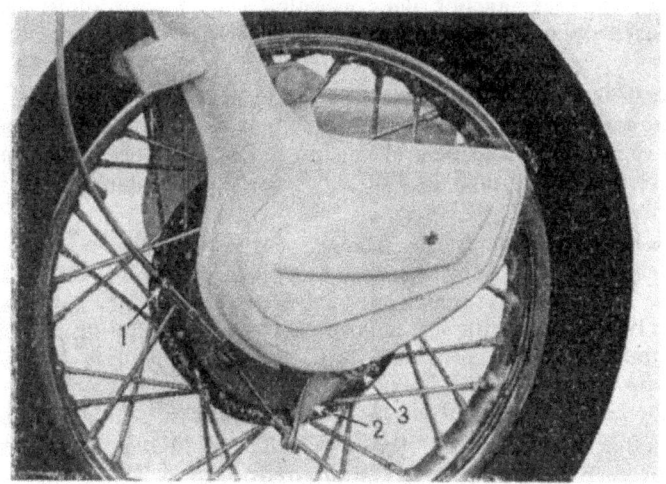

FIG. 31. NEAR SIDE OF FRONT WHEEL SHOWING BRAKE ADJUSTMENT
1. Brake adjuster sleeve.
2. Brake operating arm.
3. Nut and spring washer securing (2) to brake anchor plate.

chaincase and lift the chaincase clear. When replacing the chaincase be careful not to damage the contact-breaker oil seal and fit a new chaincase joint gasket unless the old gasket is perfect.

BRAKES, WHEELS, TYRES

Front Brake Adjustment. Keep the front brake adjusted so that the brake linings are *just* clear of the brake drum. With the machine on its centre stand and the front wheel raised it should be possible to spin the front wheel without the brake offering any friction. Make the necessary adjustment by means of the cable adjuster-sleeve positioned in the cable near the brake operating arm. Adjust until the wheel cannot be rotated, and then readjust in the opposite direction a little at a time until it is just possible to spin the wheel freely.

After a big mileage no further adjustment by means of the brake cable adjuster sleeve may be possible. In this case screw the cable adjuster sleeve right in until no threads are showing and remove the nut and spring washer securing the brake operating arm to the brake anchor plate. Remove the operating arm from the brake cam spindle and observe the serration of the operating arm relative to the square of the brake cam spindle. Replace the operating arm, moving it radially anticlockwise to the next serration. Replace the spring washer and the nut and firmly secure the operating arm in its new position. On refitting the brake cable slide the loose ferrule along the cable and refit the end soldered ferrule only into the brake anchor plate operating arm. Finally adjust the front brake carefully by means of the cable adjuster sleeve.

Rear Brake Adjustment. Adjust by means of the knurled thumb nut on the rear brake rod until the rear wheel cannot be rotated with the machine on its centre stand and neutral engaged. Then readjust in the opposite direction a little at a time until the wheel can just be rotated freely.

Adjustment on Some Earlier Models. On some earlier models a nylon brake-shoe fulcrum adjuster is screwed into the brake plate of both wheels. The adjuster is square ended and fitted instead of the later hexagon-headed bolt, and is on the side opposite to the brake operating arm. Where a fulcrum adjuster is provided, turn the squared end of the adjuster *clockwise* until the brake lining is just rubbing the brake drum. Then turn the adjuster *anticlockwise* at least five "clicks." Finally adjust the cable adjuster sleeve on the front brake or the thumb nut on the rear brake.

Altering Rear Brake Pedal Position. To suit individual riders the brake pedal position can be altered. A stop pin on the brake pedal boss determines the position of the brake pedal relative to the nearside footrest. Position the brake pedal as required by slackening off the thumb nut on the brake rod and screwing the stop pin up or down as needed, after loosening its lock-nut. Afterwards tighten the lock-nut and carefully adjust the brake. Further adjustment of the brake pedal position can be made by loosening the pinch-bolt securing the brake operating lever on the offside of the machine to the serrated cross shaft and fitting the lever in a different position. Make sure that movement of the operating lever does not cause the lever to foul the gearbox. Finally tighten the pinch-bolt, adjust the brake pedal stop pin, and adjust the rear brake as required.

Fierceness of Braking. This is generally caused through bad brake adjustment or through dust collecting from brake lining wear. In the latter case it is necessary to remove the brake assembly and clean out

GENERAL MAINTENANCE

all dust, etc. If the lining becomes worn down almost to the rivet heads, exchange shoes and linings should be fitted.

To Remove the Rear Brake Pedal. To remove the pedal (necessary when dismantling the primary chaincase) slacken the pinch bolt and remove the brake rod operating lever from the off side of the splined cross shaft. Then from the near side withdraw the brake pedal with its integral cross shaft. Clean the cross shaft and grease liberally before replacing it.

The Wheel Bearings. The wheel bearings of both wheels are non-adjustable and if adequately lubricated (*see* page 25) should give trouble-free service.

To Remove Front Wheel. Position the machine on its centre stand and remove the cover plate from the outer side of each fork leg. A single fixing screw secures each cover plate. Unscrew the screw until it floats freely. A retaining rubber keeps the screw in the plate which should be moved forward about half an inch and lifted clear. Disconnect the brake cable from its operating arm. Slacken the cable adjuster located about two inches from the operating arm; pull the cable to the rear and lift the cable outer cover from the operating arm; then move the inner cable forward to slide the nipple from the slotted stop on the brake anchor plate.

Where the brake has a triangular torque arm bracket on the brake anchor plate the brake cable outer cover is fitted in the slotted stop and the cable nipple is fitted in the operating arm. Remove as previously described. If a fulcrum adjustment is provided, screw out the adjuster a few turns in an *anticlockwise* direction and remove the cable.

Remove the bolt and special lock-nut which secure the brake torque arm to the bottom of the offside fork leg. Note the two semi-spherical washers which are fitted to protect the special torque arm pivot bearings. Do not remove the slotted nut which secures the brake torque arm to the brake anchor plate.

On a machine which has the torque arm attached to a triangular bracket on the brake anchor plate remove the bolt and nut securing the torque arm to the bracket. Do not undo the bolt which secures the torque arm to the fork leg, or the bolt and nut which secure the triangular bracket to the brake anchor plate.

Before removing the wheel spindle compress the hydraulic units slightly and keep them compressed by inserting, one at each side, the two $\frac{1}{4}$ in. diameter rods supplied in the tool kit of each new machine. The rods must pass through the holes in the fork stanchions and engage the hole in the light alloy trailing link. To compress the hydraulic units no great effort is normally required.

Remove the nut securing the wheel spindle on the offside, slacken the spindle pinch bolt and withdraw the wheel spindle. A tight spindle should be removed with a service withdrawal tool. Then remove the front wheel. Do not remove the rods which keep the hydraulic units compressed. Keep these in position until the wheel is replaced.

On the grounds of safety a front stand (Part No. T2151) should be fitted before withdrawing the wheel spindle. Alternatively a strong box or support about six and a half inches high should be placed under the forward end of the exhaust pipes. On no account lower the fork legs to ground level or the centre stand will spring up and the machine overturn.

Removal of Front Brake Plate. When occasion is had to remove the front wheel remove the brake plate and inspect the brake linings for wear. To remove the plate, slide it off the bearing sleeve. It is important not to allow brake lining wear to become so extensive that a lining securing rivet can score the brake drum.

Replacing Front Wheel. Pass the front wheel between the fork legs and align the hub with the links. Then push the wheel spindle through the near-side fork link and the hub. The service withdrawal tool can be used if necessary. Align the spindle with the bush in the off-side fork link and push the spindle right through. Do not use excessive force. Where considerable resistance occurs check the alignment of the spindle and the fork link bush. As soon as enough of the spindle threaded portion projects through the off-side fork link, fit the spindle nut. This will draw the spindle right through the hub. After tightening the spindle nut check that the brake anchor plate is quite free. A tight plate can upset the action of the front suspension.

Remove the two $\frac{1}{4}$-in. diameter rods which keep the hydraulic units compressed *before* tightening the spindle pinch bolt. Also check that the near-side fork leg has not become displaced during the fitting of the wheel spindle. If it has, ease the fork leg back by using a piece of wood as a lever between the hub and the fork leg. To ensure that alignment is correct move the forks up and down several times. Tighten the pinch bolt nut after first making sure that the flat on the bolt head is parallel with the flat on the trailing link. Grease lightly the spherical torque arm bearings, and replace the brake torque arm with the dust covers and the correct bolt and self-locking nut. Tighten this nut securely. Replace both cover plates and fit and adjust the brake cable.

To Remove Rear Wheel (Leader). The tail portion of the machine hinges upwards to assist removal of the quickly detachable wheel. It is not necessary to disturb the secondary chaincase, the wheel sprocket, or the secondary chain.

With the Leader on its centre stand, loosen the two acorn nuts at the silencer end bracket so as to free the silencers from the bracket. Also slacken the two large chromium-plated pivot bolts located at the front

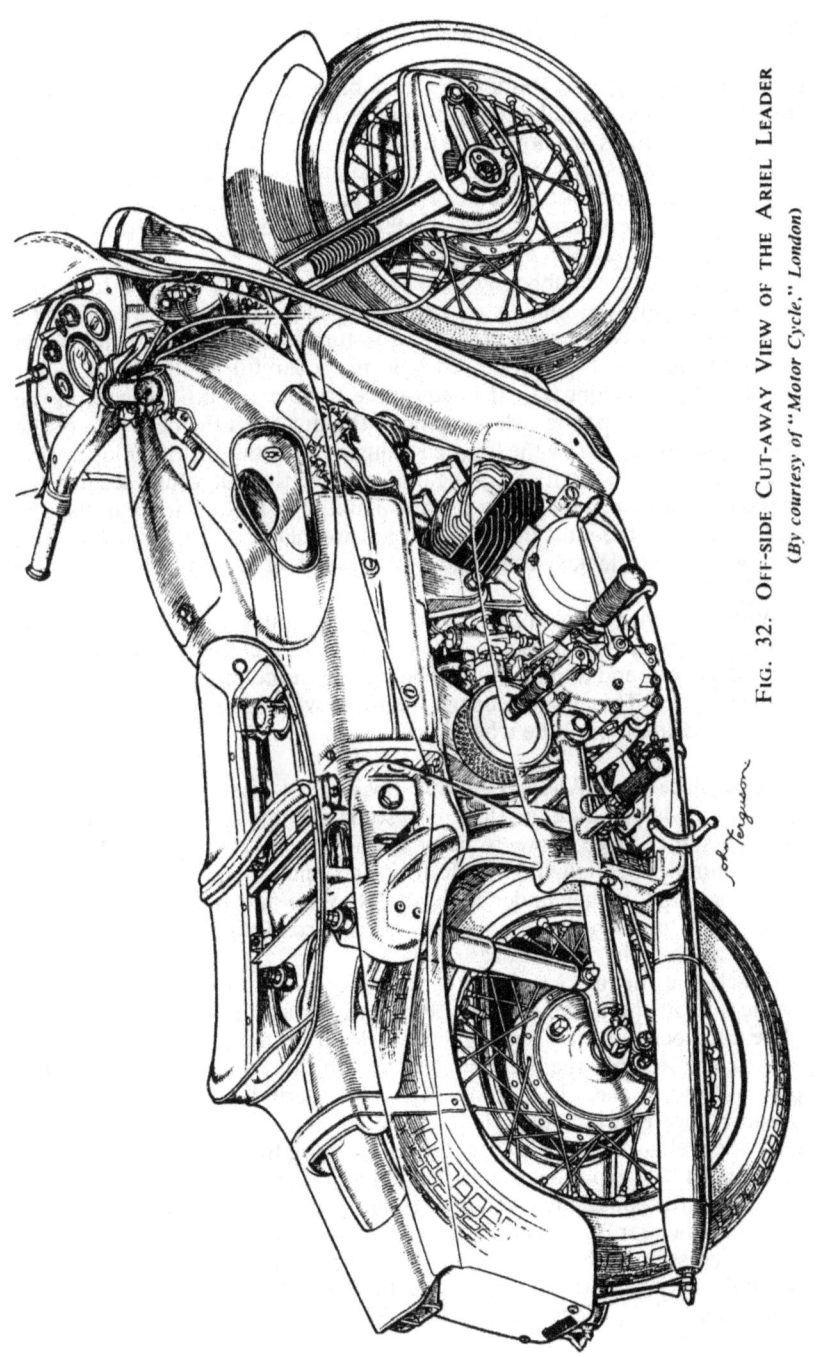

Fig. 32. Off-side Cut-away View of the Ariel Leader
(*By courtesy of "Motor Cycle," London*)

end of the tail portion. Remove the two brass wing nuts which are accessible from under the tail portion through the cavity behind the tool tray. Assuming panniers are not fitted, the tail portion can then be pivoted up.

Where panniers are fitted slacken the bolt which secures a bracket behind the forward bottom end of each pannier. The tail portion, complete with panniers, can then be pivoted up. Ease the lower front end of the tail portion past the pannier brackets.

Remove the large rubber grummet shown at (2) in Fig. 30 from the secondary chaincase and extract the nuts from the three wheel studs, turning the rear wheel so that each nut in turn lines up with the hole from which the grummet was removed. Be most careful not to allow a nut to fall into the chaincase. It is advisable to smear a little grease on the inside of the box spanner. Now remove the nut from the near side of the wheel spindle. Unscrew the knurled adjuster nut from the brake-operating rod on the offside of the machine and remove the nut which secures the brake torque arm to the brake anchor plate. The torque arm can then be pulled clear of the stud in the brake anchor plate, and the anchor plate can be rotated clockwise until the brake rod is clear of the operating arm.

Withdraw the wheel spindle, which incorporates a small tommy-bar, from the offside. Also remove the spindle distance piece fitted between the offside fork end and the hub. Then move the complete wheel sideways to the offside. This will disengage the three wheel studs from the driving sprocket. Finally pull the wheel clear.

To Replace Rear Wheel (Leader). Position the rear wheel between the rear fork ends and ease the three hub studs into the sprocket holes. Next fit the distance piece between the offside fork end and the hub. Push the wheel spindle through the offside fork end and the hub. Do not forget to fit the large washer under its head. Replace and tighten securely and evenly the three wheel-securing nuts, afterwards fitting the rubber grummet to the hole in the chaincase.

Check that the brake rod spring is positioned on the brake rod adjacent to the nut, fit the brake rod into the operating arm by rotating the brake plate anticlockwise, and replace the knurled adjuster nut on the end of the brake rod. Replace the brake torque arm on the stud in the brake anchor plate. Now fit the wheel spindle nut after verifying that the spindle is properly located in the off-side fork end. To ensure correct chain tension and wheel alignment make sure when tightening the spindle nut that there is no space between the secondary chain adjusters and the spindle. When tightening the spindle nut keep the tommy-bar in a vertical position.

Adjust the rear brake and fit and securely tighten the washer and special nut which secures the torque arm to the brake anchor plate. Then lower the tail portion of the machine and fit and tighten the pivot bolts, the wing nuts and the silencer acorn nuts. Where panniers are provided locate the two bolts which were loosened behind the panniers in the brackets and securely tighten.

To Remove Rear Wheel (Arrow). With the machine on its centre stand remove the large rubber grummet shown at (2) in Fig. 30 from the secondary chaincase and remove the three wheel stud nuts, rotating the rear wheel so that each nut in turn lines up with the grummet hole. Be careful not to allow a nut to fall into the chaincase. It is advisable to smear a little grease on the box spanner. Next remove the wheel spindle nut fitted on the near side. It is not necessary to disturb the secondary chaincase, the wheel sprocket, or the secondary chain.

FIG. 33. OFF-SIDE VIEW OF REAR WHEEL ON THE ARROW

Unscrew the knurled adjuster nut from the brake operating rod on the offside of the machine and remove the nut which secures the brake torque arm to the brake anchor plate. The torque arm can then be pulled clear of the stud in the brake anchor plate, and the anchor plate can be rotated clockwise until the brake rod is clear of the operating arm.

Withdraw the wheel spindle, which incorporates a small tommy-bar, from the off side. Also remove the spindle distance piece fitted between the off-side fork end and the hub. Then move the complete wheel sideways to the off side. This will disengage the three wheel studs from the driving sprocket. Finally lean the machine over to one side and roll the wheel clear between the tail and silencer.

To Replace Rear Wheel (Arrow). Lean the machine over to one side and ease the rear wheel between the tail and silencer. Ease the three hub studs into the sprocket holes and position the wheel spindle distance piece between the off-side fork end and the hub. Push the wheel spindle through the off-side fork end, the distance piece, and the hub. A large washer must be fitted under the spindle head. Replace and tighten securely and evenly the three wheel securing nuts, afterwards fitting the rubber grummet to the hole in the chaincase.

Check that the brake rod spring is positioned on the brake rod adjacent to the nut, fit the brake rod into the operating arm by rotating the brake plate anticlockwise, and replace the knurled adjuster nut on the end of the brake rod. Replace the brake torque arm on the stud in the brake anchor plate. Now fit the wheel spindle nut after verifying that the spindle is properly located in the off-side fork end. To ensure correct chain tension and wheel alignment make sure when tightening the spindle nut that there is no space between the secondary chain adjusters and the spindle. When tightening the spindle nut keep the tommy-bar in a vertical position. Adjust the rear brake and fit and securely tighten the washer and special nut which secures the torque arm to the brake anchor plate.

The Three Nuts Securing Rear Wheel. Remove the front rubber grummet occasionally from the chaincase and check that the three nuts on the wheel studs are securely tightened.

Tyres. On a new Ariel Leader or Arrow the White-wall tyres have a protective coating. To remove this, wash with warm water. Never use petrol for any purpose on the tyres. To keep the white side walls of the tyres clean, use a special cleaning pad, obtainable from an Ariel dealer. A free sample is provided with a new machine. Remove oil and tar stains with carbon tetrachloride or similar proprietary tar removers.

Tyre Inflation Pressures. Tyre inflation pressures slowly but surely decline even if the tyres and valves are in good condition. Always keep the valve caps screwed on tightly and check the inflation pressures of both tyres regularly by using a suitable pressure gauge such as the Dunlop pencil-type No. 6, the Schrader No. 7750, the Romac, or the Holdtite. By keeping tyre pressures correct, tyre deflection is reduced to the minimum, and maximum comfort, tyre life, and freedom from skidding are assured. Always maintain the wheels in true alignment and keep oil off the treads. On a Leader or Arrow the correct tyre pressures are—

Front tyre: 18 lb per sq in.
Rear tyre (solo): 25 lb per sq in.
Rear tyre (with pillion passenger): 28 lb per sq in.

STEERING HEAD AND FRONT FORKS

Steering Head Adjustment (Leader). The steering head bearings are of the cup and cone type and are grease packed during initial assembly.

GENERAL MAINTENANCE

Infrequent adjustment is necessary but on a new machine after covering several thousand miles some bearing wear often develops and this should be corrected by means of the adjustment provided. When the steering head is properly adjusted the front forks must pivot quite freely without any rock or play at the steering head. It is best to remove the front wheel in order to check the adjustment. With the forks pointing straight ahead, hold the two fork legs with both hands and try to move the fork legs backwards and forwards. If any rock or play is felt adjust as described below.

First take out the separate centre piece of the parcels compartment lining. This pulls out, leaving a hole which provides access to the inside of the frame. Leave the main lining in position. Next remove the anti-thief steering-head lock inside the front of the parcels compartment. The lock is secured to the frame by two bolts which pass through the frame from the inside, with the heads of the bolts welded to a common plate, and with nuts and washers securing the lock to the bolts. To remove the lock take off the two nuts and washers from inside the parcels compartment and simultaneously pass one hand inside the frame to prevent the plate dropping as you remove the nuts which secure the lock. Now remove the complete lock from the parcels compartment.

You need not remove the anti-thief steering head lock but its removal facilitates steering head adjustment. Remove the pinch bolt and nut which secure the handlebar unit to the top of the steering column and withdraw it from the steering column splines. Lay the complete handlebar assembly on the instrument panel. Remove the large rubber grummet which is visible after removing the handlebars. Visible through the grummet hole is an alloy die casting and below this is a spacer washer and two thin nuts, all mounted on the steering column. The alloy die casting is part of the anti-thief steering head lock, and together with the spacer washer they must be moved up the steering column about half an inch. Steering head adjustment can now be made by means of the two thin nuts. With one spanner hold the lower nut to prevent it turning, and with another spanner slacken the top nut by turning it *anticlockwise*. Then turn the lower nut *clockwise* until the front forks pivot quite freely, but without any play in the steering head. Be careful not to tighten the lower nut excessively, as this can damage the bearings. If the front wheel is not removed when checking the steering head adjustment, place a box beneath the crankcase to clear the wheel of the ground. After making the necessary adjustment tighten the top nut down securely while holding the lower nut with a spanner to prevent it turning.

When replacing the handlebar unit, see that it is properly located on the steering column with the front wheel pointing straight ahead. Replace the pinch bolt and nut and tighten the nut firmly. When replacing the anti-thief steering head lock first pass inside the frame the plate with the two bolts welded to it, and locate the bolts through the holes. Complete the reassembly in the reverse order of dismantling.

Steering Head Adjustment (Arrow). The steering head bearings, as on the Leader, are of the cup and cone type and need infrequent adjustment. Check the adjustment as previously described for the Leader. Where an adjustment is needed, first remove the bolt from each side of the Lucas headlamp, and allow the headlamp to hang on its harness. Remove the pinch bolt and nut from the handlebar stem bracket and withdraw the handlebars from the serrated steering column. Lay the handlebars on the front shell after covering the latter with a suitable cloth. Next remove the tool-box and remove the two nuts and bolts which pass through the brackets securing the forward end of the front shell to the top of the frame. Slacken the four screws passing through the bottom edge of the front shell. Slip the plastic cover off the steering column and lift the front shell enough to permit of access to the two thin nuts provided for steering head adjustment. Make the adjustment as previously described for the Leader. Reassembly is straightforward.

Slip the plastic cover over the steering column and replace the handlebars. Fit the pinch bolt to the handlebar stem bracket and replace the spring washer and nut. Tighten the latter securely. Tighten the four screws at the bottom of the front shell and fit the two bolts and nuts through the brackets inside the forward end of the front shell. Under each bolt head there should be a plain washer, and under each nut a shakeproof washer. Replace the tool-box and headlamp. See that a plain washer is fitted under the heads of the bolts securing the headlamp and that the distance piece is fitted between each side of the headlamp and the front shell.

The Front Forks. No maintenance is necessary except to attend to correct lubrication (*see* page 26). The hydraulic units and the suspension springs are completely enclosed in the fork stanchions and are fully protected. The light-alloy trailing links, concealed within the fork stanchions, have bushes at the forward end and these are packed with grease during initial assembly. No further attention is needed except at thorough overhaul when the old grease should be removed and the bearings packed with fresh grease. Do not forget to apply the grease gun every 1,000 miles to the grease nipples provided and indicated in the lubrication chart on page 21.

INDEX

ACCESSORY firms. 47
Air filter, 36
Alternator, 37, 59
Ariel—
   Arrow, 3
   clutch, 60
   handlebars, 5
   Leader, 1

BATTERY—
   cells, topping-up, 39
   terminal connexions, 40
Brake—
   adjustment, 65
   pedal position, 66
Brakes, use of, 17

CARBON deposits, removing, 55
Carburettor—
   assembling, 34
   cleaning, 33
   controls, 27
   dismantling, 31
   functioning, 27
   removal, 31
   replacing, 35
   settings, 28
Chaincase removal. 64
Cleaning—
   carburettor, 33
   contacts, 52
   machine, 47
   sparking plugs, 51
Clutch—
   adjustment, 61
   slip, 60
Cold-starting unit removal, 33
Contact-breaker—
   adjustment, 52
   cover, 53
   removal, 53
Contacts, cleaning. 52
Controls, 8

Cylinder—
   barrel, removal. 55
   barrels, replacing. 58
   head removal, 54
   heads, fitting, 59

DECARBONIZING, 54–9
Difficulty in starting up, 14
Dualseat, 5

ELECTRIC horn, 44
Enamelled surfaces, retouching, 48
Engine cover, 49
Exhaust system—
   removing, 54
   replacing, 59

FLASHER lamps, 42
Front brake adjustment, 65
Front forks, 74
Front wheel removal, 67
Fuel economy, 18

GAP, sparking plug. 50
Gear changing, 15
Gearbox, 60

HEADLAMP, 40–2
Horn, 44

IGNITION—
   coils, 52
   timing, 53

LEGAL preliminaries, 5
Lighting switch positions, 42
Lubrication—
   chart, 20
   system, petroil, 20
Lucas headlamp, 40–2

MAJOR engine overhaul, 59

OPTIONAL extras, 3

PARCEL compartment, 4
Petroil lubrication system, 20
Piston rings, 57
Pistons—
  fitting, 58
  removing, 55
Primary chain adjustment, 62

REAR—
  brake adjustment, 66
  brake pedal removal, 67
  wheel removal, 68, 71
Repairs and spares, 47
Replenishing fuel tank, 10
Running-in, 18

SECONDARY chain adjustment, 62
Side panels, removing, 48
Silencers, 57
Slow-running adjustment, 29
Small-end bushes, 60

Sparking plug gap, 50
Sparking plugs—
  cleaning, 51
  suitable, 50
Starting up, 13
Steering head adjustment, 72–4
Stop-tail light, 42
Stopping machine, 17

TESTING sparking plugs, 52
Throttle cable adjustment, 29
Timing, ignition, 53
Topping-up battery cells, 39
Tyres, 72

WARNING lights, 44
Wheel—
  alignment, 64
  bearings, 67
  removal and replacement, 67–72
Wiring of equipment, 44
Worn cylinders, 59

ARE YOU:
INTERESTED IN EUROPEAN, IMPORT & EXOTIC AUTOMOBILES?

DO YOU:
DO YOUR OWN MAINTENANCE?

If you answered yes to either of these questions, then you should check out our automobile books and manuals. We have included a sample listing of some of our featured marques. However, for complete details and the most up-to-date information, please visit our website.

——— www.VelocePress.com ———

The fastest growing specialist USA publisher of niche market automotive books and manuals.

All VelocePress titles are available through your local independent bookseller, Amazon.com or direct from VelocePress. Wholesale customers may also purchase direct or from the Ingram Book Group.

AUTOBOOKS WORKSHOP MANUALS

ALFA ROMEO GIULIA 1300, 1600, 1750, 2000 1962-1978 WSM
AUSTIN HEALEY SPRITE, MG MIDGET 1958-1980 WSM
BMW 1600 1966-1973 WSM
BMW 2000 & 2002 1966-1976 WSM
BMW 2500, 2800, 3.0 & 3.3 1968-1977 WSM
BMW 316, 320, 320i 1975-1977 WSM
BMW 518, 520, 520i 1973-1981 WSM
FIAT 1100, 1100D, 1100R & 1200 1957-1969 WSM
FIAT 124 1966-1974 WSM
FIAT 124 SPORT 1966-1975 WSM
FIAT 125 & 125 SPECIAL 1967-1973 WSM
FIAT 126, 126L, 126 DV, 126/650 & 126/650 DV 1972-1982 WSM
FIAT 127 SALOON, SPECIAL & SPORT, 900, 1050 1971-1981 WSM
FIAT 128 1969-1982 WSM
FIAT 1300, 1500 1961-1967 WSM
FIAT 131 MIRAFIORI 1975-1982 WSM
FIAT 132 1972-1982 WSM
FIAT 500 1957-1973 WSM
FIAT 600, 600D & MULTIPLA 1955-1969 WSM
FIAT 850 1964-1972 WSM
JAGUAR E-TYPE 1961-1972 WSM
JAGUAR MK 1, 2 1955-1969 WSM
JAGUAR S TYPE, 420 1963-1968 WSM
JAGUAR XK 120, 140, 150 MK 7, 8, 9 1948-1961 WSM
LAND ROVER 1, 2 1948-1961 WSM
MERCEDES-BENZ 190 1959-1968 WSM
MERCEDES-BENZ 220/8 WSM
MERCEDES-BENZ 220B 1959-1965 WSM
MERCEDES-BENZ 230 1963-1968 WSM
MERCEDES-BENZ 250 1968-1972 WSM
MERCEDES-BENZ 280 1968-1972 WSM
MG MIDGET TA-TF 1936-1955 WSM
MINI 1959-1980 WSM
MORRIS MINOR 1952-1971 WSM
PEUGEOT 404 1960-1975 WSM
PORSCHE 911 1964-1973 WSM
PORSCHE 911 1970-1977 WSM
RENAULT 16 1965-1979 WSM
RENAULT 8, 10, 1100 1962-1971 WSM
ROVER 3500, 3500S 1968-1976 WSM
SUNBEAM RAPIER, ALPINE 1955-1965 WSM
TRIUMPH SPITFIRE, GT6, VITESSE 1962-1968 WSM
TRIUMPH TR2, TR3, TR3A 1952-1962 WSM
TRIUMPH TR4, TR4A 1961-1967 WSM
VOLKSWAGEN BEETLE 1968-1977 WSM

BROOKLANDS BOOKS & ROAD TEST PORTFOLIOS (RTP)

AC CARS 1904-2009
ALFA ROMEO 1920-1933 ROAD TEST PORTFOLIO
ALFA ROMEO 1934-1940 ROAD TEST PORTFOLIO
BRABHAM RALT HONDA THE RON TAURANAC STORY
BUGATTI TYPE 10 TO TYPE 40 ROAD TEST PORTFOLIO
BUGATTI TYPE 10 TO TYPE 251 ROAD TEST PORTFOLIO
BUGATTI TYPE 41 TO TYPE 55 ROAD TEST PORTFOLIO
BUGATTI TYPE 57 TO TYPE 251 ROAD TEST PORTFOLIO
DELAHAYE ROAD TEST PORTFOLIO
FERRARI ROAD CARS 1946-1956 ROAD TEST PORTFOLIO
FIAT 500 1936-1972 ROAD TEST PORTFOLIO
FIAT DINO ROAD TEST PORTFOLIO
HISPANO SUIZA ROAD TEST PORTFOLIO
HONDA ST1100/ST1300 PAN EUROPEAN 1990-2002 RTP
JAGUAR MK1 & MK2 ROAD TEST PORTFOLIO
LOTUS CORTINA ROAD TEST PORTFOLIO
MV AGUSTA F4 750 & 1000 1997-2007 ROAD TEST PORTFOLIO
TATRA CARS ROAD TEST PORTFOLIO

VELOCEPRESS AUTOMOBILE BOOKS & MANUALS

ABARTH BUYERS GUIDE
AUSTIN-HEALEY 6-CYLINDER WSM
BMW 600 LIMOUSINE FACTORY WSM
BMW 600 LIMOUSINE OWNERS HAND BOOK & SERVICE MANUAL
BMW ISETTA FACTORY WSM
BOOK OF THE CARRERA PANAMERICANA - MEXICAN ROAD RACE
DIALED IN - THE JAN OPPERMAN STORY
FERRARI 250/GT SERVICE AND MAINTENANCE
FERRARI 308 SERIES BUYER'S AND OWNER'S GUIDE
FERRARI BERLINETTA LUSSO
FERRARI BROCHURES AND SALES LITERATURE 1946-1967
FERRARI BROCHURES AND SALES LITERATURE 1968-1989
FERRARI GUIDE TO PERFORMANCE
FERRARI OPP, MAINTENANCE & SERVICE H/BOOKS 1948-1963
FERRARI OWNER'S HANDBOOK
FERRARI SERIAL NUMBERS PART I - ODD NUMBERS TO 21399
FERRARI SERIAL NUMBERS PART II - EVEN NUMBERS TO 1050
FERRARI SPYDER CALIFORNIA
FERRARI TUNING TIPS & MAINTENANCE TECHNIQUES
HOW TO BUILD A FIBERGLASS CAR
HOW TO BUILD A RACING CAR
IF HEMINGWAY HAD WRITTEN A RACING NOVEL
JAGUAR E-TYPE 3.8 & 4.2 WSM
LE MANS 24 (THE BOOK THAT THE FILM WAS BASED ON)
MASERATI BROCHURES AND SALES LITERATURE
MASERATI OWNER'S HANDBOOK
METROPOLITAN FACTORY WSM
MGA & MGB OWNERS HANDBOOK & WSM
OBERT'S FIAT GUIDE
PERFORMANCE TUNING THE SUNBEAM TIGER
PORSCHE 356 1948-1965 WSM
PORSCHE 912 WSM
SOUPING THE VOLKSWAGEN
TRIUMPH TR2, TR3, TR4 1953-1965 WSM
VEDA ORR'S NEW REVISED HOT ROD PICTORIAL
VOLKSWAGEN TRANSPORTER, TRUCKS, STATION WAGONS WSM
VOLVO 1944-1968 ALL MODELS WSM

VELOCEPRESS MOTORCYCLE BOOKS & MANUALS

AJS SINGLES 1955-65 350cc & 500cc (BOOK OF)
ARIEL 1939-1960 4 STROKE SINGLES (BOOK OF)
ARIEL LEADER & ARROW 1958-1964 (BOOK OF)
ARIEL MOTORCYCLES 1933-1951 BOOK
ARIEL PREWAR MODELS 1932-1939 (BOOK OF)
BMW M/CYCLES R26 R27 (1956-1967) FACTORY WSM
BMW M/CYCLES R50 R50S R60 R69S (1955-1969) FACTORY WSM
BSA BANTAM (BOOK OF)
BSA OHV & SV SINGLES - 250cc 1954-1970 (BOOK OF)
BSA OHV & SV SINGLES 1945-54 250-600cc (BOOK OF)
BSA OHV SINGLES 350 & 500cc 1955-1967 (BOOK OF)
BSA PREWAR MODELS TO 1939 (BOOK OF)
BSA TWINS 1948-1962 (BOOK OF)
BSA TWINS 1962-1969 (SECOND BOOK OF)
DUCATI 160cc, 250cc & 350cc OHC MODELS FACTORY WSM
HONDA 50 ALL MODELS UP TO 1970 (BOOK OF)
HONDA 90 ALL MODELS UP TO 1966 (BOOK OF)
HONDA MOTORCYCLES 125-150 TWINS C/CS/CB/CA WSM
HONDA MOTORCYCLES 250-305 TWINS C/CS/CB WSM
HONDA MOTORCYCLES C100 SUPER CUB WSM
HONDA MOTORCYCLES C110 SPORT CUB 1962-1969 WSM
HONDA TWINS & SINGLES 50cc to 305cc 1960-1966 (BOOK OF)
LAMBRETTA ALL 125 & 150cc MODELS 1947-1957 (BOOK OF)
LAMBRETTA LI & TV MODELS 1957-1970 (SECOND BOOK OF)
MATCHLESS 350 & 500cc SINGLES 1945-1956 (BOOK OF)
MATCHLESS 350 & 500cc SINGLES 1955-1966 (BOOK OF)
NORTON 1938-1956 (BOOK OF)
NORTON DOMINATOR TWINS 1955-1965 (BOOK OF)
NORTON MOTORCYCLES 1957-1970 FACTORY WSM
NORTON PREWAR MODELS 1932-1939 (BOOK OF)
ROYAL ENFIELD 736cc INTERCEPTOR FACTORY WSM
ROYAL ENFIELD 250cc & 350cc SINGLES 1958-1966 (SECOND BOOK OF)
SUZUKI 50cc & 80cc UP TO 1966 (BOOK OF)
SUZUKI T10 1963-1967 FACTORY WSM
SUZUKI T20 & T200 1965-1969 FACTORY WSM
TRIUMPH MOTORCYCLE 1935-1939 (BOOK OF)
TRIUMPH MOTORCYCLES 1937-1951 WSM
TRIUMPH MOTORCYCLES 1945-1955 FACTORY WSM
TRIUMPH TWINS 1956-1969 (BOOK OF)
VELOCETTE ALL SINGLES & TWINS 1925-1970 (BOOK OF)
VESPA 1951-1961 (BOOK OF)
VINCENT MOTORCYCLES 1935-1955 WSM

www.VelocePress.com

Please check our website:

www.VelocePress.com

for a complete up-to-date list of available titles

www.ingramcontent.com/pod-product-compliance
Lightning Source LLC
Chambersburg PA
CBHW070602170426
43201CB00012B/1906